CRITICAL STUDIES OF
KEY TEXTS

Virginia Woolf's
To the Lighthouse

Suzanne Raitt

*Queen Mary and
Westfield College, London*

HARVESTER
WHEATSHEAF

New York   London   Toronto   Sydney   Tokyo   Singapore

First published 1990 by
Harvester Wheatsheaf
66 Wood Lane End, Hemel Hempstead
Hertfordshire HP2 4RG
A division of
Simon & Schuster International Group

Typeset in 10½/12pt Sabon
by Inforum Typesetting, Portsmouth

Printed and bound in Great Britain by
Billing and Sons Limited, Worcester

British Library Cataloguing in Publication Data

Raitt, Suzanne, *1961–*
  To the lighthouse.
  I. Title
  823.912
  ISBN 0–7108–1369–4

---

1 2 3 4 5   94 93 92 91 90

Contents

Contents

Note on the Text

To the Lighthouse was first published by Leonard and Virginia Woolf at the Hogarth Press in 1927. Corrections that Virginia Woolf made to the Hogarth proofs were incorporated in the American edition of the novel, which came out later in the same year with Harcourt, Brace & World; these corrections have never been included in the British edition to date. The edition that I refer to throughout this book is the paperback Triad/Grafton *To the Lighthouse*, which was first published in London in 1977.

Acknowledgements

I should like to thank the following for their help and encouragement with this project: Liz Bellamy, Gillian Beer, Teresa Brennan, and Caroline Kay. I am very grateful to Mary Hamer, Stephen Heath, Janet Hiddleston, Diana Hinds and Sandra Kemp for reading and commenting on drafts of this book. Many of the ideas I present here were worked out in the context of the Cambridge feminist literary theory group. I thank particularly Liz Goodman, Sarah Maguire, Paulina Palmer, Helen Small, and Sophie Tomlinson, for their help and support.

I am grateful to the Master and Fellows of Gonville and Caius College, Cambridge, for awarding me a Research Fellowship, which enabled me to carry out the research for this book and offer acknowledgement to the British Academy for awarding me a small research grant to assist with this project.

Acknowledgement is made to the Executors of the Virginia Woolf Estate, and the Hogarth Press, for permission to reprint extracts from Virginia Woolf's diary, and *To the Lighthouse*. I am grateful to Harcourt Brace Jovanovich for permission to reprint the following in the United States: excerpts from *To the Lighthouse* by Virginia Woolf, copyright 1927 by Harcourt Brace Jovanovich, Inc., and renewed 1955 by Leonard Woolf, reprinted by permission of the publisher. Excerpts from *The Diary of Virginia Woolf*, Volume III, copyright © 1980 by Anne Olivier Bell, Quentin Bell, Angelica Garnett, reprinted by permission of Harcourt Brace Jovanovich, Inc.

Abbreviations

Preface

The French critic Hélène Cixous has written, 'it is impossible to *define* a feminine practice of writing, and this is an impossibility that will remain, for this practice can never be theorized, enclosed, coded – which doesn't mean that it doesn't exist.'[1] The task of feminist criticism is to struggle with this maddening intangibility. Conviction – that a feminine writing *does* exist – is not enough. Feminism is about analysis and action, the demand to know. What is it that makes female humans into women? What are the conditions of women's lives and identities? And, for feminist criticism, what is the significance of the relation between women and the texts that they write?

Different nations and different cultures produce their own distinctive feminist idioms. Feminist criticism in the United States has paid much attention to the economic and social conditions of women writing; in France the emphasis has been on the relation between text and sexuality; in Britain there has been concern with the relation between class and the oppression of women. Different theoretical models, some of which this book will outline, encourage differing insights. We only see what we are looking for, which is why, for so long, we read canonical texts as if they had nothing specific to say to women.

To the Lighthouse is a novel that is fascinated by women. The perspectives of Mrs Ramsay and Lily are the most fully developed, and the lengthiest, narratives in the novel. *To the*

Preface

Lighthouse is an obvious text for feminist critics to choose to write about, since it takes up questions of the sexuality of women, women's role in the family, motherhood and daughterhood. But it devotes equal energy to the question of the woman artist (Lily), to the nature of the artistic gaze (what kind of attention does a painter give to his/her model?) and the dynamics of the relation between a woman artist and her female model, when the model happens to be, in the words of the novel, 'famous for her beauty' (TL, 52).

In looking for ways of understanding these dynamics I have at points turned to film theory and its feminist developments. Although much of this is abstruse and difficult, there are some basic insights which are helpful in the analysis of the politics of the look in the novel. Of course Lily Briscoe is not just looking: she is painting as well. Nor is she watching a film. But nonetheless she is transfixed, like women in the cinema, by a woman whose beauty is legendary. Some key concepts in film theory – identification for example – are also used in psychoanalytic accounts of the mother–daughter relationship in which Mrs Ramsay and Lily, after a fashion, participate. Film theory offers a way of understanding Lily both as spectator and as daughter, and of comparing her reactions with those of the men who are also caught up in admiration of Mrs Ramsay's beauty. The coincidence of Lily's roles both as daughter, and as woman looking at and representing woman, is the unsolved problem of the novel.

A slim book such as this cannot do justice to a text as complex as *To the Lighthouse*. In concentrating on Lily and Mrs Ramsay I have had inevitably to pass over some other aspects of the novel. But I hope I have drawn attention to at least some of its innovatory strategies. However, there is always work left to do.

I

Contexts

Historical and Cultural Context

'The cruel thing was that while we could see the future, we were completely in the power of the past' (SP, 147). In her appraisal of her life, written when she was in her fifties, Virginia Woolf described her adolescence at the turn of the century as an experience of personal and cultural transition. She had felt in thrall to the 'complete model of Victorian society' (SP, 148) maintained at her London home of 22 Hyde Park Gate, whilst being 'by nature' one of her own generation's 'explorers, revolutionists, reformers' (SP, 147). This dichotomy fuelled a 'violent struggle' both with the men who ruled her home and, more lastingly, within her own mind and imagination (SP, 147). It was a particular brand of Victorianism that offered her the freedom to experience, and then to analyse, such feelings of intellectual conflict. In the mornings, the young Virginia Stephen studied Greek and Latin for her twice-weekly lessons with Janet Case, and roamed her father Leslie Stephen's library with no restrictions at all on what she might read. The confidence that this gave her in her own judgement meant that she rebelled silently against Stephen's domestic tyranny during his lifetime, and rejected altogether his attitude to sexual relations and the family after his death in 1904.

Woolf's immediate social milieu, at least in the years just following her father's death, is now famous as the Bloomsbury group. The precise composition of this group, and the dates at which it flourished, are disputed – even the two

Woolfs disagree. This lack of clarity reflects the fact that, as Virginia's husband Leonard Woolf noted, the term was usually 'applied to a largely imaginary group of persons with largely imaginary objects and characteristics'.[1] Virginia Woolf more confidently describes its beginnings as being in the Thursday evening parties she, her sister Vanessa Bell (then Stephen) and their brother Adrian gave at their house in Gordon Square between 1904 and 1906, the year their Cambridge brother Thoby died (OB, 190). Virginia mentions among the guests Saxon Sydney-Turner, Lytton Strachey, Clive Bell and Leonard Woolf (OB, 190). Both Woolfs mention the influence of Cambridge philosopher G. E. Moore. Despite the claim sometimes made that the Bloomsbury group was devoted to, and spent hours in serious discussion of, Moore's work, his influence seems to have been most marked in his effect on their interest in, and conduct of, their personal relations. Moore believed that aesthetic enjoyment and friendship were the two most important pleasures in life, and his emphasis on absolute candour licensed conversations of great intellectual frankness and informality among the friends who met at Gordon Square. Beyond that, according to Leonard Woolf, there was no adherence to 'a common doctrine and object, or purpose artistic or social',[2] and Virginia, in her memoir, stressed the disputatious nature of their meetings. The evenings were unpredictable. At first, 'one could stumble off to bed feeling that something very important had happened' (OB, 194). Later, the evenings were 'always strained and often ended in dismal failure' (OB, 198). But the silences and the unpredictability were themselves exciting; such social risks would never have been taken in Virginia Woolf's father's drawing-room.

Later, after Vanessa's marriage to Clive Bell in 1907, intellectual frankness was extended to include a measure of sexual openness. When Lytton Strachey uttered the word 'semen', 'a flood of the sacred fluid seemed to overwhelm us' (OB, 200). The resultant energetic debate meant that 'the old sentimental views of marriage in which we were brought up were revolutionised' (OB, 201). From these hours of 'rapt interest' (OB, 201) emerged the mature Woolf who would write *To the Lighthouse* as a meditation on marriage, its charm and its challenge. The restlessness of Hyde Park Gate and the discussions of Gordon Square produced a mind which could be at once nostalgic and self-critical, and which sought a prose style that would allow the greatest possible intellectual and emotional honesty: one whose mature complexity would match the complexity of its author's dilemmas.

All of Woolf's revolutions were achieved by talking and listening. 'Talk – even the talk which had such tremendous results upon the lives and characters of the two Miss Stephens – even talk of this interest and importance is as elusive as smoke', she mourns, nearly twenty years later (OB, 190). Bloomsbury's attachment to the private transaction gives a certain smugness to this remark (Woolf originally delivered 'Old Bloomsbury' as a lecture to a dining club composed mostly of those old friends who had participated in the talk so many years before). This smugness signals the particular position of Bloomsbury within the class system of which it was at times so severely critical. What Bloomsbury challenged was a Victorian sense of obligation and duty, 'all that tremendous encumbrance of appearance and behaviour' (OB, 194) which had so oppressed the young Virginia Stephen. Domestic and social imperatives no longer held. The rejection of 'old sentimental views' (OB, 201) which Woolf mentioned involved a change in what one expected of oneself, as well as in what others expected of one. It was not necessarily a revolution which demanded active political affiliation with the disadvantaged. It was a revolution in outlook, forcing reassessments – of imperialism, of the class system – which remained, for Woolf at any rate, matters of conscience only. Raymond Williams wrote of Bloomsbury:

> What has most carefully to be defined is the specific association of what are really quite unchanged class feelings – a persistent sense of a quite clear line between an upper and a lower class –

with very strong and effective feelings of sympathy with the
lower class as victims.[3]

Woolf continues to have difficulty with imaginative empa-
thies outside the Bloomsbury paradigm of the intimate transaction, of talk by the middle-class fire. Faced with a roomful
of working-class women, she balks at their 'passive sort of
pleasure in sitting there & watching like so many pale grey
sea anemones stuck to their rocks. Still, the children, the
housework – excuses enough if one troubled to look' (D, I, 23
January 1918, 112). It is in the 'troubling to look' that the
social becomes the political conscience. Woolf's insouciant
laziness ('*if* one troubled to look' [my italics]) throws into
sharper relief the boundaries of the effort she is prepared to
make. The talk round the fire to which she is committed
indicates a privileged excess of intellectual energy. Her social
conscience as it is presented in this diary entry is a matter of
idle speculation, an intellectual and emotional indulgence.

It is from this kind of 'explorer, revolutionist, reformer'
that the experiments of her later fiction derive. In 1924 Virginia Woolf imagined asking a question of her Edwardian
novelist predecessors, Bennett, Wells and Galsworthy:

How shall I begin to describe this woman's character? And they
said: 'Begin by saying that her father kept a shop in Harrogate.
Ascertain the rent. Ascertain the wages of shop assistants in the
year 1878. Discover what her mother died of. Describe cancer.
Describe calico. Describe' – But I cried: 'Stop! Stop!'[4]

What Woolf rejects is the conscientious effort of the Edwardian novel, and its antecedents in the Victorian period (Charles
Dickens, the industrial novel of the 1840s, George Eliot) to
record the whole spectrum of a society in the process of
change, through the accumulation of accurate factual detail.
Mrs Ramsay is mocked for this kind of desire in *To the Lighthouse*. She notes down the finances of the households she
visits:

in the hope that thus she would cease to be a private woman
whose charity was half a sop to her own indignation, half a

relief to her own curiosity, and become, what with her un-
trained mind she greatly admired, an investigator, elucidating
the social problem. (TL, 14)

Mrs Ramsay's mimicking of a social investigator is touching
and absurd because her carefully ruled notebooks remain
simply a personal record. Her statistics bear witness to her
own emotions – her desire, half-narcissistic, to become a public figure – rather than to any wider understanding of social
policy.

It was towards the kind of prose that could simultaneously
articulate desire and the material detail – Mrs Ramsay's little
notebooks – that Woolf aspired. Her description of a society
in crisis, in 'Time Passes', the central section of *To the Lighthouse*, hardly mentions the war which darkens both its pages
and the history of a civilisation. (Jane Austen, one of Woolf's
most admired authors, is famous for a similar omission in
Pride and Prejudice, 1813.) The crisis in 'Time Passes' is one
of image, of symbol: the disquieting absence of character and
historical personality. In this kind of experiment, Woolf felt
herself to be part of a historical tradition that reached back
beyond the Edwardians to writers such as Laurence Sterne,
and the Elizabethans. But she also identified, at least in part,
with contemporary innovations in fiction. Despite their differences, she had a sense of common purpose with Katherine
Mansfield. On 2 June 1920 they had '2 hours priceless talk –
priceless in the sense that to no one else can I talk in the same
disembodied way about writing' (D, II, 5 June 1920, 45). It
was apparently to a suggestion of Mansfield's that Woolf
owed the idea for one of her earliest experimental pieces, *Kew
Gardens* (1919). Woolf also thought highly of the work of
James Joyce and Dorothy Richardson. Joyce, she wrote, was
'concerned at all costs to reveal the flickerings of that inner-
most flame which flashes its messages through the brain', and
Dorothy Richardson is praised for inventing 'the psychological sentence of the feminine gender'.[5] But both are privately
criticised for allowing the 'damned egotistical self' (D, II, 26
January 1920, 14) to ruin their work; the style for which

Woolf was striving would be to 'record the atoms as they fall upon the mind' in a way that revealed more than simply a personal vision.[6]

Yet it was precisely the serenity and clarity of the personal vision to which she clung. The complexity of her reactions to the General Strike of 1926 – during which she wrote 'Time Passes' – shows her struggling to preserve her peace of mind. She assisted Leonard in collecting signatures to a petition demanding fair treatment of reinstated miners after the settlement of the strike, but her distress and resentment at the upheaval the strike caused in her life are written into 'Time Passes', as Kate Flint has shown.[7] Virginia and Leonard quarrelled: 'I dislike the tub thumper in him: he the irrational Xtian [Christian] in me' (D, III, 9 May 1926, 80–1). The political process irked her: 'what one prays for is God: the King or God; some impartial person to say kiss & be friends – as apparently we all desire' (D, III, 6 May 1926, 78). As always, she was irritated by the minutiae of historical change. Even her arguments against the oppression of women are couched in terms of the damage their suffering does to the acuity of their artistic vision:

> we feel the influence of fear in [Charlotte Brontë's portrait of Rochester in *Jane Eyre*], just as we constantly feel an acidity which is the result of oppression, a buried suffering smouldering beneath [Brontë's] passion, a rancour which contracts those books, splendid as they are, with a spasm of pain.[8]

It was in terms of her own 'buried suffering' that she wrote her novel of the First World War, *To the Lighthouse*. The agony of her war was a peculiarly private one, born of and breeding isolation. Following her marriage in 1912, she suffered prolonged periods of mental disturbance which continued until the end of 1915. Leonard Woolf wrote that the years from 1914 to 1918 were dominated as much by Virginia Woolf's illness, and slow recovery, as by the war. Virginia's breakdown was linked to her mother's early death in 1895. During one relapse, in March 1915, she suddenly 'thought her mother was in the room and began to talk to her.'[9] She reacted to the personal crisis of her marriage, and the national crisis of 1914–18, by revisiting her first trauma: the death of her mother. In her distress at her country's suffering she seemed to experience her primary bereavement for the second time. As we shall see, Mrs Ramsay is closely modelled on the mother with whom Woolf was obsessed to the point of madness during the war years.

In retrospect, Woolf saw *To the Lighthouse* as a form of therapy: a text with a peculiar relation to her own history, which functioned for her as a psychical and emotional release. Having completed *To the Lighthouse* in 1926, she went on to write the fantasy–biography *Orlando* (1928), a celebration of her friend and former lover, Vita Sackville-West. She continued to experiment with biography in *The Waves* (1931), which follows the lives of six friends through six monologues which repeatedly interrupt and reply to each other. *The Years* (1937) was an experiment in realism along the lines of Galsworthy's *The Forsyte Saga* published between 1906 and 1921. But Woolf was deeply discontented with it, and before the final revisions of her next novel, *Between the Acts* (1941), she drowned herself in the Sussex Ouse.

Critical Reception of the Text

From the 1930s to the present day, *To the Lighthouse* has enjoyed a favoured position in criticism of Woolf's works. Even the group of critics associated with the Cambridge journal *Scrutiny*, who lampooned Woolf's books during the 1930s, singled out *To the Lighthouse* as her best novel. The publication in the 1970s of biographical material associated with Woolf prompted an even greater critical emphasis on *To the Lighthouse*. With the insights gained from Woolf's diaries, her autobiographical essays and her letters, it became possible to analyse *To the Lighthouse* as autobiographical fiction, and to speculate about its function in Woolf's beleaguered psychical life.

The reliance of *To the Lighthouse* on details of Woolf's own life – her recreation of her parents, of her childhood summers in Cornwall and, most importantly, of her mother's early death – makes it a pivotal moment in Woolf's *œuvre*. It is the text in which her life and her writing come together most directly and most problematically. *To the Lighthouse* focuses interest on Woolf's life as a context for her work, on her narrative techniques, and on her criticism of conventions of sexual difference.

On the day of publication of *To the Lighthouse* (5 May 1927) Woolf wrote in her diary that she found herself:

> in the shadow of the damp cloud of the Times Lit Sup. review, which is an exact copy of the JsR. [*Jacob's Room*] Mrs Dalloway review, gentlemanly, kindly, timid & praising beauty,

doubting character, & leaving me moderately depressed. I am anxious about Time Passes. Think the whole thing may be pronounced soft, shallow, insipid, sentimental. (D, III, 134)

The *Times Literary Supplement* reviewer had noted the novel's plotlessness, suggested that 'the meaning of things . . . is not only the essence but the real protagonist in the story', and commented on 'the charm and pleasure of the design'.[1] However, he pronounced 'Time Passes' weaker than the rest, and this was an opinion that was echoed by Arnold Bennett in the *Evening Standard* (23 June 1927), and Edwin Muir in the *Nation and Athenaeum* (2 July 1927). But reviews were generally favourable, if cautious and slightly puzzled. Orlo Williams in the *Monthly Criterion* of July 1927 summed up the critics' dilemma: 'for imaginative prose of this kind there ought to be another name, since it is a thing different from the novel, verging at its most exalted moments on poetry.'[2] Despite the critics' reservations, *To the Lighthouse* won the Prix Femina in 1928 and sales, while falling short of the success the Hogarth Press would subsequently achieve with *The Years*, were good.

Woolf's major critical setback occurred in the 1930s with the growth of Fascism and the emergence of a politicised young generation. Where Rachel Taylor had said in 1927 that in *To the Lighthouse*, 'nothing happens, and everything happens', later reviewers, and particularly the *Scrutiny* group, were convinced only that nothing had happened.[3] Woolf was attacked for the privilege of her class position and her apparent lack of social and political imagination. Muriel Bradbrook criticised Woolf's lack of commitment and the evasive nature of her narrative style. (Recently Bradbrook refused permission to reprint the article, saying she had changed her mind.)[4] Later, *To the Lighthouse* was singled out by Mellers and Leavis as the only good novel in an *œuvre* of 'extraordinary vacancy and pointlessness': by Mellers in 1937 on the grounds that in this novel at least something happens (the trip to the lighthouse); by Leavis in 1942 because its closeness to autobiography prevented it from degenerating too far into abstraction.[5] The most sustained attack on Woolf's work, though, came in Queenie Leavis's review of *Three Guineas* (1938), Woolf's feminist pamphlet. She accuses Woolf of inaccuracy, self-indulgence and political short-sightedness.[6] This anger – backed up from a different quarter by the venom of Wyndham Lewis's satire in *Apes of God* (1930) – set the terms of the debate over Woolf's work not only for that decade, but for much of its ensuing history. Winifred Holtby (*Virginia Woolf*, 1932) defended Woolf's intellectual candour; David Daiches in *The Novel and the Modern World* (Chicago, 1939), while critical of Woolf for 'remaining in her study', insisted that in *To the Lighthouse* the rarefied atmosphere was right and appropriate for what she had to say. The issue of whether or not Woolf's fiction was socially and politically engaged enlivened – or bogged down – Woolf studies for decades to come, and opened the door to a feminist appropriation of her work in the 1970s and 1980s.

Virginia Woolf died in 1941. In E. M. Forster's celebration of his dead friend in the Leslie Stephen lecture of 1942, he claimed that she had 'pushed the light of the English language a little further against darkness.'[7] As the decade progressed, a couple of other critics also began to pay closer attention to the language of her work. In England, Joan Bennett, in *Virginia Woolf: Her art as a novelist* (Cambridge, 1945), announced that the effacement of the author in Woolf's books was not a refusal to commit herself, as Bradbrook had thought, but a sign of Woolf's sympathetic, rather than judgemental, attitude towards her characters. From Switzerland Erich Auerbach in the now classic *Mimesis* (published 1946, translated 1953) produced a superb piece of analysis of narrative point of view in *To the Lighthouse* that set Woolf's narrative technique firmly on the agenda for Woolf criticism.

The publication of extracts from Woolf's diary, *A Writer's Diary*, in 1953 gave added confidence to critical work on Woolf. The Marxist Arnold Kettle continued the Leavisite tradition from another angle by complaining that *To the Lighthouse* was 'not about anything very interesting or important', but it was by that time established enough as an academic text for him to include it in his *An Introduction to the English Novel* (New York, 1951).[8] James Hafley, in *The Glass Roof: Virginia Woolf as novelist* (1954), turned his attention to Woolf's ideas (implicitly disagreeing with Bradbrook's remark that 'to demand "thinking" from Mrs. Woolf is clearly illegitimate').[9]

During the 1950s Mrs Ramsay began to emerge as a major focus of attention and controversy. (The publicity given to psychologist D. W. Winnicott's work on the mother–child relationship during these years is surely not a simple coincidence.) Joseph Blotner, in his reading of *To the Lighthouse* as a commentary on the myth of Persephone, maintained that Mrs Ramsay was 'the meaning of the novel', and 'a symbol of the female principle in life'.[10] But Glenn Pedersen, two years later, singled out Mrs Ramsay for a blistering attack, accusing her of refusing 'to subordinate her individuality to community', and of thus condemning her family to isolation and disruption.[11] Gradually the critical emphasis switched from class to domestic politics – both being arguments whose ideological implications extended, and still extend, far beyond this single novel. The passionate concern of critics such as Blotner and Pedersen with the nature of mature femininity would be developed in later years by many other Woolf scholars.

Criticism in the 1960s continued to debate Mrs Ramsay and how far she succeeds in fulfilling her domestic role, but critics also grew more interested in the context of *To the Lighthouse* and in its links to its sister arts of painting and music (Woolf's sister Vanessa Bell and her lover Duncan Grant were both professional artists). In 1967 Keith May looked at painting in the novel, and in 1968 Harold Fromm showed that its emotional effects were similar to those of music.[12] Allied to this exploration of the novel's links with arts other than literature was a growing interest in the novel's symbolism (see, for example, N. C. Thakur, *The Symbolism of Virginia Woolf*, London, 1965), and in Woolf's vision of the world (Susan Rubinow Gorsky, in *Virginia Woolf,*

Boston, 1978, decided she was fundamentally despairing). Jean Guiguet's monumental *Virginia Woolf and her Works* (1962) and Schaefer's *The Three-Fold Nature of Reality in the Novels of Virginia Woolf* (London, 1965) consider the relation between form and content in Woolf's novels. Both books are concerned to demonstrate the intricate connection between Mrs Ramsay and the lighthouse.

The simultaneous appearance in 1970 of the Macmillan Casebook volume on *To the Lighthouse* edited by Morris Beja, and Thomas Vogler's collection, *Twentieth-Century Interpretations of 'To the Lighthouse'* (Englewood Cliffs, 1970), confirmed *To the Lighthouse* as a canonical text for schools and universities. In the same year, Mitchell Leaska brought out a painstaking formalist analysis of the text, developing Auerbach's insights with an at times algebraic precision (*Virginia Woolf's Lighthouse: A study in critical method*), and Geoffrey Hartman, in his essay 'Virginia's Web', offered a deconstructionist reading, linking the artist's resistance to her own vision to resistance and warning as themes in the novel.[13]

With the publication of Quentin Bell's biography of his aunt in 1972, and the gradual release of many volumes of Woolf's private papers (the letters appeared between 1975 and 1980, and the diaries between 1977 and 1984), criticism of Woolf took off. Dozens of volumes appeared during the 1970s and 1980s, along with numerous articles. Some continued to address well-established topics; others opened up new ground for debate.

In 1972 two feminist contributions to Woolf studies were published. Annis Pratt analysed the sexual imagery of *To the Lighthouse*, and noted the 'distorted elements in [Mrs Ramsay's] sexual relations' (suggestions of phallic imagery in connection with her sexuality).[14] However, Pratt explicitly denies that Woolf intends a critique of gender relations as they are usually maintained, insisting that Woolf was deliberately describing an untypical relationship. This was not a view that would be endorsed by Pratt's feminist successors.

Criticism in the mid-1970s tended to concentrate on themes of conflict and synthesis in Woolf's work. Alice van Buren Kelley (*The Novels of Virginia Woolf: Fact and vision*, Chicago, 1973), Nancy Topping Bazin (*Virginia Woolf and the Androgynous Vision*, New Brunswick, 1973) and Jane Novak (*The Razor Edge of Balance: A study of Virginia Woolf*, Miami, 1974) all continued Carolyn Heilbrun's work on androgyny as a critical term to describe the recognition and transcendence of difference (*Toward a Recognition of Androgyny*, New York, 1964).

In 1977 the relationship between Lily and Mrs Ramsay – hitherto rather passed over, even by critics like Annis Pratt, in favour of analysis of the Ramsays' marriage – became a central focus for discussion. Ruddick and Lilienfeld both drew on autobiographical material (*Moments of Being*, a collection of Woolf's autobiographical essays, had appeared in 1976) to explore the treatment of the powerful mother figure in the text.[15] At the same time, Leaska followed up his formalist analysis of *To the Lighthouse* with some gibes at Mrs Ramsay, in *The Novels of Virginia Woolf: From beginning to end* (New York, 1977). Delia Donahue, refreshingly irreverent, criticised all the solemn psychoanalysing that had become part of the picture of *To the Lighthouse* criticism after the publication of Woolf's private papers:

> The critics note at once: 'Ha ha! The Oedipus complex!' By doing so they discover nothing and make nothing clearer. To liken these childish impulses [James Ramsay's] to the violent and incestuous Oedipus is as grossly to exaggerate as if one were to describe as Hamletic doubt one's indecision whether to take bus No. 3 or bus No. 9.[16]

Phyllis Rose's 1978 biography, *Woman of Letters: A life of Virginia Woolf*, continues undaunted Ruddick and Lilienfeld's work on Lily/Woolf's ambivalence towards the mother figure, and raises questions about the construction of gender in both Woolf's life and in *To the Lighthouse*. In 1979, Robert Caserio was one of the first to bring together issues of domestic politics and narrative structure in his work on genealogies and narrative logic in *To the Lighthouse*.[17] Gayatri Chakravorty Spivak continues this in a 1980 article on the copula and copulation in *To the Lighthouse*.[18] In the same year Maria Dibattista, in her study of anonymity in Woolf's work, called *To the Lighthouse* Woolf's 'masterwork on the Victorian family romance'.[19] Mark Spilka (*Virginia Woolf's Quarrel with Grieving*, 1980) made an abrupt about-turn in biographical criticism of the novel, suggesting that it bore marks of repression and, implicitly, of a failure of courage, in its omission of some of the salient facts of Woolf's own childhood (her mother's first marriage, for example). He considers *To the Lighthouse* to be only a partial working-through of her grief at her mother's death, and a demonstration of Woolf's inability to come to terms with the traumas of her childhood and adolescence.

In 1981, Jane Marcus emerged as a central figure in US feminist criticism of Virginia Woolf, with the publication of her first collection of essays about the sexual politics of Woolf's novels (*New Feminist Essays on Virginia Woolf*). This was followed in 1983 by another collection, *Virginia Woolf: A feminist slant*, in which Woolf's private papers are used to demonstrate the radical Virginia that she repressed from the public texts. Howard Harper (*Between Language and Silence: The novels of Virginia Woolf*, London, 1982) was dismissive of the relevance of Woolf's life and her recently published letters and diaries for understanding the novels, and traced the evolution of Woolf's consciousness through her fictional texts instead. Madeline Moore (*The Short Season between Two Silences: The mystical and the political in the novels of Virginia Woolf*, London, 1984) also suggested a slightly different direction for feminist criticism to take, rejecting materialist analysis in favour of an examination of Woolf's presentation of affective states, and suggesting that Lily's real radicalism lies in her creation of a more challenging kind of love that that of Mrs Ramsay, which tends to reinforce the status quo.

Lyndall Gordon published a biography of Virginia Woolf in 1984 (*Virginia Woolf: A writer's life*, Oxford). In it, Gordon uses *To the Lighthouse* extensively to trace the genesis of Woolf's creative gift, and suggests that in writing this novel, Woolf achieved command over her parents and control of her own writing talent. Gillian Beer considers *To the Lighthouse* as a work of mourning, and looks at the influence of the philosophy of David Hume and Leslie Stephen on the development of the novel.[20]

David Dowling continued the tradition of linking *To the Lighthouse* with visual art forms in his study of Woolf's interest in the aesthetic theories of Roger Fry and Charles Mauron (*Bloomsbury Aesthetics and the Novels of Virginia Woolf*, London, 1985). This contextualising approach in Woolf studies increasingly took the form of a return to more materialist biographical criticism. Alex Zwerdling (*Virginia Woolf and the Real World*, Berkeley, 1986) describes *To the Lighthouse* as a critique of Victorian domestic life, paying considerable attention to the autobiographical context while pointing out the differences between Woolf's own story and that of the Ramsays. Kate Flint takes the General Strike of 1926 as a context for the writing of 'Time Passes', the central section of *To the Lighthouse*, in an attempt to situate Woolf's political thought in a national, rather than a domestic context.[21]

To the Lighthouse appears as the typical modernist text in Juliet Dusinberre's *Alice to the Lighthouse* (Basingstoke, 1987), which studies the shift in consciousness exemplified in children's changing reading habits. Again, *To the Lighthouse* is taken to represent Woolf's achievement of power over her parents (much as Lyndall Gordon had described), and her development of a modernist world view.

Two of the most recent studies of Woolf's novels re-emphasise the importance of psychoanalytic theory for an understanding of her work. Makiko Minow-Pinkney (*Virginia Woolf and the Problem of the Subject*, 1987) uses Kristevan theory to discuss gender in Woolf's novels, whilst

Rachel Bowlby (*Virginia Woolf: Feminist destinations*, 1988) returns to Freudian paradigms to look at the construction of masculinity and femininity in the novels. The latest study of *To the Lighthouse*, Stevie Davies' *Virginia Woolf: 'To the Lighthouse'* (Harmondsworth, 1989), shows how the novel continues the tradition of classical elegy and uses the metaphor of the sea to explore the rhythms of life and death.

A radical reinterpretation of Virginia Woolf's life came in Louise DeSalvo's *Virginia Woolf: The impact of childhood sexual abuse* (London, 1989). Piecing together fragments from Woolf's published and unpublished manuscripts, DeSalvo argues that Woolf was not occasionally, but repeatedly, abused by her brothers, and that her work and ensuing emotional difficulties should be understood in this context. Brilliantly argued, this controversial book has aroused debate not only about Virginia Woolf, but also about sexual abuse, and about the aims of feminist criticism and its attitudes towards the lives of the women whose work it reads.

In all this wealth of discussion there has been little attempt to link *To the Lighthouse* with any of Woolf's non-fiction, other than *A Room of One's Own* (1929) and *Three Guineas* (1938). These texts can be used to show that Lily's task as an artist is to achieve androgyny, as *A Room of One's Own* advises, and that her strategic refusal, at various points in the book, to come to the rescue of men, is a deliberate withdrawal along the lines of the 'Outsider Society' described in *Three Guineas*.

These are not the only links to be made between *To the Lighthouse* and Woolf's non-fiction. Vital ones exist, for example, between *To the Lighthouse* and a little-read essay by Woolf, 'The cinema', which she was working on while she wrote *To the Lighthouse*. This book will document those links and develop them to produce a reading of *To the Lighthouse* that acknowledges its contribution to a culture of which the film industry was an increasingly important part. It would not be possible to produce such an analysis were it not for the work of Julia Kristeva, Makiko Minow-Pinkney and

Rachel Bowlby; and in the area of film studies, of Laura Mulvey and Mary Ann Doane. The following section will explain how theoretical work can open up new areas of attention in apparently exhausted texts.

Theoretical Perspectives

Criticism of *To the Lighthouse* has often had an axe to grind. In the previous section we noted Bradbrook's observation that 'to demand "thinking" from Mrs. Woolf is clearly illegitimate.'[1] Bradbrook, however, immediately makes her own views on what she perceived as Woolf's intellectual vagueness abundantly clear. 'Such a deliberate repudiation of [thinking] and such a smoke screen of feminine charm is surely to be deprecated', she growls.[2] Feminine charm is often at issue in criticism of *To the Lighthouse*. Pedersen, as we saw, finds Mrs Ramsay extremely un-charming. He is enraged at the arrangement of the family in the first section of the book:

> the father should not be outside the window, looking at the mother and son in the window; the husband and wife should be together, the son with them both, but not between them, and most of all, not between the mother's knees.[3]

Horrors. Pedersen's holy family has been disturbed by the monstrous figure at its centre: the 'Madame Defarge' that is Mrs Ramsay, 'not sympathising but laughing and knitting'.[4]

Neither of these two critics would claim for themselves a specific theoretical perspective. Indeed *Scrutiny*, the journal in whose opening issue Bradbrook's article appeared, implicitly rejected any notion of theory. In a model of criticism that reaches back to Matthew Arnold's belief that culture preserves the moral fibre of a nation, the editors of *Scrutiny* described their aim as the encouragement of a 'play of the free intelligence upon the underlying issues', believing also that 'there is a necessary relationship between the quality of the individual's response to art and his general fitness for a humane existence'.[5] This bracing notion depended on a direct and unfettered meeting of critic and text, in which intelligence was entirely free to play upon the issues of its choice. Any theoretical model – a prescribed vocabulary organising a reader's response to the text – would contaminate the purity of the critical encounter.

Glenn Pedersen, similarly, has no need of theory. His version of the healthy family is so self-evidently clear to him that he assumes the reader will share his understanding of Mrs Ramsay's monstrosity. His criticism does not proceed by argument, or even by very close analysis of the text: it is enough for him merely to assert his point of view.

These two examples of an untheoretical approach to the text both operate according to strictly defined systems of values – the moral function of criticism, or the iniquity of the wife who fails to respond to her husband's demands for sympathy. These systems of values are simply taken for granted in the criticism. We might call this not a theoretical perspective, but an ideological one, which presents a particular belief system as natural and universal. The role of theory in criticism of *To the Lighthouse* has been to investigate assumptions such as these which lie not only behind the novel itself, but also behind much of its criticism. Theory has attempted to undo the effects of ideology by exposing the ways in which particular beliefs are silently incorporated into a text and presented not as beliefs at all, but as *facts*. A psychoanalytic critic might say of Glenn Pedersen's article that it itself bore traces of Pedersen's own Oedipal conflict, in his anger against James for monopolising his mother's attention.

The development of theoretical vocabularies – whether they be Bloomian, Freudian, or Derridean – makes it possible to talk about areas of meaning which have previously remained unexpressed. Analysis of narrative elements according to the schemes suggested by Propp or Genette can help us understand how narrative works, and what it is we unconsciously expect from, and find in, stories. The movement into theory is a way of producing a criticism that is aware of its own unconscious assumptions, as well as those of the text it studies. This awareness does not necessarily involve the dismantling of all beliefs, or the end to any moral or political impetus in criticism; rather it can help us to understand and define our own attitudes and objectives. Psychoanalytic criticism in particular can lead to an increased comprehension of the involvement of memory and fantasy with our conscious perceptions and our critical activities. Ideally this produces a criticism with a keener persuasive edge and a moral and political framework which is apparent from the start, and carefully enunciated throughout the piece of work.

It will already be clear from the previous section, 'Critical Reception of the Text', that *To the Lighthouse* has been at the centre of many political and theoretical debates. As we saw, much of the early criticism seemed to have a mission to judge the novel and its characters: Mr and Mrs Ramsay are alternately praised and condemned, condemned and praised. This early ideological criticism has given way in more recent years to a psychoanalytically based criticism with allegiances to various psychoanalytic schools, such as those of Freud, Klein and Lacan. Often, psychoanalytic language has been used by feminist critics as a way of discussing how gender is constructed in the text. In these cases, it has an explicit political aim: to demonstrate that gender difference is maintained to the disadvantage of women, and, in the most recent work, to show that it is in relationships with other women that women find much of their support and energy. The marriage between psychoanalytic and feminist perspectives has been a most fruitful one for criticism of *To the Lighthouse*.

To the Lighthouse has attracted very little Marxist or socialist criticism. One exception is Arnold Kettle's 1953 essay, which concluded that the novel was 'not about anything very interesting or important'.[6] This exclusion of the novel from the Marxist literary project is a conscious political strategy. In pointing out that *To the Lighthouse* restricts itself to the representation of the lives and problems of the upper middle class, Kettle shows how the novel strengthens the dominance of the upper over the lower classes by presenting the world from the former's point of view. More recently, however, Michèle Barrett has produced a materialist feminist account of Woolf's non-fiction which suggests that Woolf saw the root of women's oppression in their economic situation. Woolf, she says, 'argued that the writer was the product of her or his historical circumstances, and that material conditions were of crucial importance.'[7] But in Barrett's view, Woolf would also constantly resist the implications of her own analysis, holding on to the idea of a 'pure' art emancipated from the constraints of material conditions, which should be the aim of all practising writers.

To the Lighthouse is a novel about memory and desire. Lily's grieving appeal ('to want and not to have, sent all up her body a hardness, a hollowness, a strain' [TL, 165]) is at the heart of the book, and is paralleled by other versions of remembering, of wanting and of loss. This has encouraged theoretical approaches to the novel that are also concerned to analyse the articulation and narration of desire. Primary among these is the theoretical vocabulary of psychoanalysis. Psychoanalysis in all its forms assumes that a person's childhood memories, whether or not they are conscious, determine his or her personality. Since most children grow up in a family setting, so the family is crucial to psychoanalytic understandings of normal and abnormal development. Freud's model for the child's development – involving a pre-Oedipal phase when the child is only aware of its mother, followed by the development, and passing, of the Oedipus complex, through which the child tries to come to terms with his or her relations to both parents – assumes that children grow up with both their parents. Even where this does not occur, the Oedipal model can still be used to plot trauma and assist recovery. *To the Lighthouse*, which concentrates on one family and all the different relationships occurring within it – as well as a few more occurring outside it, but still mesmerised by it (Lily, Tansley and Bankes all thinking about the Ramsays) – is a text that offers all the raw material psychoanalytic critics need. They have not been slow to respond.

One of the earliest examples of a Freudian approach is Perry Meisel's study of Woolf's relations with the Victorian writer Walter Pater (*The Absent Father*, 1980). Meisel draws on the theories of the American critic Harold Bloom to argue that Woolf's apparent lack of interest in Pater – she barely mentions him in print – demonstrates his importance to her as a precursor.

Harold Bloom's vision, first articulated in *The Anxiety of Influence* (1973), was of a world in which 'the history of fruitful poetic influence . . . is a history of anxiety and self-saving caricature, of distortion, of perverse, wilful revisionism.'[8] In other words, younger poets, overawed by their predecessors, are always engaged in a bitter struggle to outdo them and to 'correct' their work. Bloom proposes a theoretical vocabulary, based on ancient Greek, to describe the ways in which poets deal with the work of their precursors. The model on which Bloom constructs his vision of 'father' and 'son' poets fighting over the muse ('mother') is the Freudian family romance, in which the son perceives himself in conflict with the father for the mother's body – her love. The Oedipus complex involves learning to forget (repress) this struggle, so that a form of reconciliation between father and son is achieved – that masculine reunion which is perhaps essential to patriarchy.

Perry Meisel, in a clever twist to this, suggests that Woolf was involved in a similar kind of Oedipal struggle with the figure of Walter Pater, and that this struggle was related to her feelings for her father and his role as Victorian man of letters and custodian of learning. Tracing a dual influence on Woolf's work, Meisel suggests a circular pattern of rivalry and reconciliation:

> having neutralised her father by arming herself with Pater, she is now able to neutralise Pater as well, by arming herself with a

politics [feminism] whose own source leads back to Stephen
[her father] to put the compensatory apparatus in motion once
again.⁹

That is, the initial disloyalty to her father implied by her
choice of Pater as a model is erased by her attack on some
aspects of Pater's work using an analytic model she learnt
from her father. The fact that Pater is barely mentioned by
Woolf, and was not liked or discussed in Bloomsbury, only
strengthens Meisel's case since, in Bloom's words, 'discontinuity is freedom. Prophets and advanced analysts alike pro-
claim discontinuity.'¹⁰

Bloom and Meisel place the Freudian grid over generations
of literary history. A more recent work on *To the Lighthouse*,
Rachel Bowlby's *Feminist Destinations* (1988), applies Freudian theory to the grouping from which it was originally derived: the two-parent family. Bowlby says that 'Woolf's
explorations of what makes the difference of the sexes are
uncannily close to Freud's'; drawing on Freud, Bowlby analyses the Ramsays' marriage as a drama in which 'Mr Ramsay
attempts to recover, with another woman, the relation of
dependence and centrality in which he once stood, or imagines he once stood, to his own mother.'¹¹ Freudian models
had of course been used before – implicitly – in criticism of *To
the Lighthouse*, Pedersen's 1958 outcry being one example.
But Bowlby's account makes explicit her reliance on Freudian
theory, defending this decision by stressing that it was the
Hogarth Press (Woolf's publisher) which brought out Freud's
work in translation, and that psychoanalysis was much discussed in Bloomsbury.

Freudian theory is useful to Bowlby and to other feminists
because it suggests reasons for the exorbitance of Ramsay's
demands on his wife, and for the struggles of both Lily and
Mrs Ramsay with the roles in which they find themselves.
Freud, in his confused and confusing account of the development of little girls, points out – perhaps inadvertently – 'the
impossibility', as Bowlby puts it, 'for "woman" of finding an
approximate identity to match – to challenge and to fit in

with – that of the masculine scenario which has already put her in certain contradictory positions'.[12] Other feminists, though, have found this emphasis on the difficulties of women's lives dispiriting. Jane Lilienfeld and Sara Ruddick prefer to use Kleinian models and the work of American psychoanalyst Nancy Chodorow, to analyse the relationship between Lily and Mrs Ramsay, assuming, as Chodorow has shown, that 'a girl retains her preoedipal tie to her mother (an intense tie involved with issues of primary identification, primary love, dependence, and separation) and builds oedipal attachments to both her mother and her father upon it.'[13] Lily – the substitute daughter – experiences her conflicts over femininity primarily in the context of her relationship with Mrs Ramsay, and for many critics it is this series of encounters which holds the key to the emerging mystery of Lily's womanhood.

Other versions of psychoanalytic theory encourage close analyses either of the structure of the text, or of its language. Gayatri Chakravorty Spivak's 1980 essay, 'Unmaking and making in *To the Lighthouse*' is 'an attempt to use the book by the deliberate superimposition of two allegories – grammatical and sexual – and by reading it, at moments, as autobiography'.[14] The dictum behind such an approach seems to be the French psychoanalyst Lacan's phrase: 'the unconscious is structured like a language'.[15] If this is true – if similar operations occur in the unconscious as occur between words in a sentence, or between sentences in a conversation – then we can analyse desire and narrative simultaneously. We could say that desire involves subjects and objects, as language does, and that the fulfilment of desire is like the function of a verb – the action of the subject on the object. Spivak offers a grammatical allegory of the structure of *To the Lighthouse*:

> The second part of the book couples or hinges I and III. In Part I, Mrs Ramsay is, in the grammatical sense, the subject [i.e. in Part I we see largely through her eyes, hear her thoughts]. In Part III, the painting predicates her [i.e. she is the object of the

painting, its predicate, and we see her only in its image of her]. I could make a grammatical allegory of the structure of the book: Subject (Mrs Ramsay) – copula – Predicate (painting).[16]

In other words, Mrs Ramsay is transformed in Part II from a seeing, speaking subject to a silent image in the painting.

The second dimension of Spivak's allegory is of course a sexual one. ' "Copulation" happens not only in language and logic, but also between persons.'[17] The structure of the book mirrors the erotic aims of various people on Mrs Ramsay: Lily seeking to possess Mrs Ramsay in her picture, and Mr Ramsay, who has 'seemingly caught her in the copula of marriage.'[18] The form and the content of the novel can thus be analysed simultaneously, and the inextricability of their connection – the perfection of the novel – demonstrated.

Spivak's version of the relation between language and desire is not particularly concerned with repression. She analyses structures and looks for coherence, rather than disruption. The last theoretical approach I want to turn to is concerned almost exclusively with the disturbance of logical sequence, whether grammatical or sexual. Makiko Minow-Pinkney (*Virginia Woolf and the Problem of the Subject*, 1987) uses the work of Julia Kristeva and her theory of the 'semiotic' – a pre-linguistic energy which, in adult discourse, erupts in rhythm, nonsense and laughter – to analyse Woolf's subversion of logical patriarchal narrative sequence. In this way she manages to link the study of Woolf's narrative technique with a close reading of her texts, and a careful account of how Woolf's feminism functioned within her actual language to upset and ridicule expectations of conformity. In doing so, she seems to answer Toril Moi's 1985 appeal for a criticism that would locate 'the politics of Woolf's writing *precisely in her textual practice*.'[19] Moi argues that Woolf's work seeks to undo gender as a transcendental category, revealing 'a deeply sceptical attitude to the male-humanist concept of an essential human identity.'[20] Moi sees gender not as a fixed entity, but as a process: 'The search for a unified individual self, or gender identity or indeed "textual identity" in the literary work must be seen as drastically reductive.'[21]

This book will start from Moi's premise that the construction of gender is an activity in which we all engage throughout our lives. Lily working on her painting is also working on herself, thinking about Mrs Ramsay and what it means to be a woman. Her obsessive stare at Mrs Ramsay helps her paint Mrs Ramsay, but it also draws her attention back to her own body and her beauty or lack of it. This book will use the psychoanalytic concepts of identification and narcissism to understand Lily's troubled gaze: 'It was then . . . as she began to paint, that there forced themselves upon her other things, her own inadequacy, her insignificance' (TL, 23). If this is the condition of female creativity, it is imperative that we bring every pressure we can to bear on its transformation.

II

To the Lighthouse:
A Reading of the Text

1

Ghosts

On 6 August 1925 Virginia Woolf began to write her fifth novel, *To the Lighthouse*. Her previous novel, *Mrs Dalloway* (1925), had, rather in the manner of Joyce's *Ulysses* (1922), described the passage of a day in London. Several characters whose paths we have followed during the day, come together at the end with the announcement of Septimus' death at Clarissa's party. *To the Lighthouse* is structured rather differently. In her notes for the novel, Woolf drew an 'H' shape and wrote above it: 'two blocks joined by a corridor.'[1] The first part of the novel, describing a summer evening before the First World War, is separated from the last part by the section called 'Time Passes'. Elsewhere in her manuscript (that is, in the one draft which has survived) Woolf called this section 'an interesting experiment, ~~showi~~ giving the sense of 10 years passing.'[2] In the last part, 'The Lighthouse', the trip that was suggested at the opening of the novel is achieved in spite of the changes and disruption caused by the passing of those years. Not only has Britain's history been darkened by the war, but the party who gathered at the Ramsays' house on Skye in the first part of the novel, 'The Window', has been reduced by death: Mrs Ramsay has died; her daughter Prue has died in childbirth; and her son Andrew has been killed in the war. Despite this, in the third part of the novel some of the remaining family members and guests return to the house. Lily finishes painting the picture she started ten years before; Mr Ramsay, with his two youngest children, arrives at the lighthouse.

The novel is constructed around an interruption. The obscenity of the deaths, the stormy chaos and darkness of the middle section, cut short the idyll of the first part and ensure that nothing will ever be quite the same again. Yet in the last part of the novel something is restored: Mr Ramsay and the children arrive at the lighthouse with an air of triumph; Lily, mourning Mrs Ramsay, imagines she sees her again and is able to finish the picture which has been causing her so much trouble. The completion of the trip and the painting in spite of Mrs Ramsay's absence seems like a denial of the abyss of loss and meaninglessness that yawned in the centre of the novel. In the chapters that follow, we shall see that the novel repeatedly uses Mrs Ramsay's image to evade its own vision of despair. The work of film critics on the cult of female screen stars will be relevant here. But in this first chapter it is necessary to examine the genesis of *To the Lighthouse*, and its connections with the events of Woolf's life.

Virginia Woolf's earliest thoughts about the novel were concerned with the theme of interruption. Before she began to write in August 1925 she had been mulling over her story for months. On 6 January 1925 she wrote in her diary:

> Here I conceive my story – but I'm always conceiving stories now. Short ones – scenes – for instance The Old Man (a character of L.S.) [Leslie Stephen, her father] The Professor on Milton – (an attempt at literary criticism) & now The Interruption, women talking alone. (D, III, 6 January 1925, 3)

Interruption will be a constant hazard in *To the Lighthouse*. Nancy and Andrew interrupt Paul and Minta kissing behind a rock; Prue runs into her parents in the middle of their walk; Lily lives in fear that someone will come and look at her canvas and break her concentration. Woolf's short story, *The Interruption*, was never written. Instead its themes, including that of the conversation of women (Lily and Mrs Ramsay in Lily's bedroom), would be incorporated into her novel.

Mr Ramsay in the boat is 'an old man, very sad, reading his book' (TL, 170). He combines in one character Woolf's 'Old

Man', her 'Professor', and her father. For her father is a brooding presence over her thoughts of the book, and her reflections on it, as we have seen. By the middle of May she was eager to begin work on *To the Lighthouse* (she already has the title).

> This is going to be fairly short: to have father's character done complete in it; & mothers [*sic*]; & St Ives; & childhood; & all the usual things I try to put in – life, death & c. But the centre is father's character, sitting in a boat, reciting We perished, each alone, while he crushes a dying mackerel – However, I must refrain. (D, III, 14 May 1925, 18–19)

For the first time in her writing career (at least her *public* career) Virginia Woolf was determined to combine recreation of events and figures from her own life with the usual preoccupations of her fiction: life and death, presence and absence.

It is unclear why, at the age of 43, she should have become so intent on recording her parents' characters and her childhood summers at Talland House in St Ives. But after the novel was written and published, she thought of it as a kind of exorcism.

> I used to think of him & mother daily; but writing The Lighthouse, laid them in my mind. And now he comes back sometimes, but differently. (I believe this to be true – that I was obsessed by them both, unhealthily; & writing of them was a necessary act.) He comes back now more as a contemporary. I must read him some day. I wonder if I can feel again, I hear his voice, I know this by heart? (D, III, 28 November 1928, 208)

Like Mrs Ramsay in *To the Lighthouse*, Leslie Stephen is still a *revenant*, but he is a *revenant* who is purged of the pathological tendency to overlook all his daughter does. If he had lived, 'his life would have entirely ended mine. What would have happened? No writing, no books; – inconceivable' (D, III, 28 November 1928, 208). The writing of *To the Lighthouse* transforms her father from intruder into visitor. Woolf, like James and Cam in the boat, finds herself finally able to forgive. Leslie Stephen, the 'contemporary', is allied to Mr

Ramsay, transformed at the end of the novel into a 'young man' (TL, 191).

Jeanne Schulkind, the editor of Woolf's autobiographical writings, believes that 'the cathartic experience of writing *To the Lighthouse*'[3] enabled Woolf to write more convincingly about her parents in her 1939–40 account of her life than she had been able to in the earlier essay (1907–8) that she had attempted before she wrote the novel. Woolf herself comments in the later piece, 'Sketch of the past', that in the novel she 'did for herself what psycho-analysts do for their patients. I expressed some very long felt and deeply felt emotion. And in expressing it I explained it and then laid it to rest' (SP, 94). The novel is, then, very close to autobiography (and Lily, perhaps, close to Woolf – Woolf drew a line down the centre of her last page of manuscript, as Lily does down her painting). Woolf was puzzled by both the genesis of *To the Lighthouse* and its effect: 'My lips seemed syllabling of their own accord as I walked. What blew the bubbles? Why then? I have no notion' (SP, 94). Woolf often used this metaphor of unconscious creation for the writing of her books. She wrote the last pages of *The Waves* 'with some moments of such intensity & intoxication that I seemed only to stumble after my own voice' (D, IV, 7 February 1931, 10). But the 'syllabling' of *To the Lighthouse* was a process of involuntary recall as well as of literary creation, and was therefore doubly unexpected for Woolf.

Woolf also disowned the effect of *To the Lighthouse* on her mental life:

> In expressing [my emotion] I explained it and then laid it to rest. But what is the meaning of 'explained' it? Why, because I described [my mother] and my feeling for her in that book, should my vision of her and my feeling for her become so much dimmer and weaker? Perhaps one of these days I shall hit on the reason. (SP, 94)

It is hard not to feel that this incomprehension on Woolf's part is disingenuous. Her checking herself – 'but what is the meaning of "explained"?' – implies that she has once again caught herself writing without full control over what she writes. Her feeling that there is some enigma about the process of literary creation is used to justify a failure to understand one of her own sentences. The mystery of fiction writing – of stumbling over voices and creating new worlds – becomes an alibi for a reluctance to extend the boundaries of self-knowledge, and makes such self-analysis a matter of chance: 'perhaps one of these days . . .'.

In her diary, Woolf describes the laying of her father's ghost by *To the Lighthouse*. In her memoirs, it is her mother's phantom which is erased: 'when it was written, I ceased to be obsessed by my mother. I no longer hear her voice; I do not see her' (SP, 94). Where her father is transformed into a less threatening *revenant*, her mother is simply written out of her life. This pattern is duplicated in *To the Lighthouse*. To put it crudely, Mr Ramsay is still alive at the end of the novel (although Leslie Stephen had in fact been dead for twenty years), and Mrs Ramsay, for all her power to disturb, is not. But more than that: the trip in the boat sees the beginning of a reassessment of James and Cam's relationships with their father ('they both wanted to say, Ask us anything and we will give it you' [TL, 190]), whereas Lily's revision of her feelings about Mrs Ramsay while painting her picture is placed unambiguously in the past tense: 'it was done; it was finished. Yes, she thought, laying down her brush in extreme fatigue, I have had my vision' (TL, 192). The revelation is over. As Woolf wrote of her mother, defiantly: 'I do not see her'. Lily's line down the centre of her painting could be simply one of erasure.

In view of the complexity with which these issues are explored in the novel, Woolf's disavowal – 'perhaps one of these days I shall hit on the reason' – seems a wilful refusal to investigate her own self-knowledge. Her novel accomplishes the obliteration of the maternal figure, and the transformation of the paternal ('he sprang, lightly like a young man' [TL, 191]) with an intensity that is very far from naïve. She knew that what she was writing was something to do with mourning: 'But while I try to write, I am making up "To the Lighthouse" – the sea is to be heard all through it. I have an idea that I will invent a new name for my books to supplant "novel". A new – by Virginia Woolf. But what? Elegy?' (D, III, 27 June 1925, 34). In her novel, and in her life, she would discover that the terms of her grief, and her recovery from that grief, for her father and her mother, were widely divergent. Perhaps it was partly this that she meant when she wrote of the end of the novel that she hoped one would have 'the sense of reading the two things [Lily finishing her picture and Mr Ramsay arriving at the lighthouse] at the same time' (D, III, 5 September 1926, 106).

Her plans for the book move between the two poles of her father and her mother. In her diary in May 1925 she wrote, as we saw, that the 'centre' would be 'father's character'; but on the first page of her manuscript, begun on 6 August 1925, she wrote that the 'dominating impression [was] to be of Mrs. R's character.'[4] The shift in emphasis is not only from her father to her mother; it is also from autobiography to fiction, from 'father' to 'Mrs R'. By the time she comes to write the first words, personal history has come to seem only the inspiration of the novel, rather than its *raison d'être*. But when the novel is finally published, she is more than happy to have it received as a form of autobiography. Her sister, Vanessa Bell, wrote to her after reading *To the Lighthouse* for the first time:

> It seemed to me that in the first part of the book you have given a portrait of mother which is more like her to me than anything I could ever have conceived of as possible. It is almost painful to have her so raised from the dead . . . . You have given father too I think as clearly but perhaps, I may be wrong, that isn't quite so difficult. (L, III, 11 May 1927, 572)

For Bell it is Mrs Ramsay, and not Mr Ramsay, who has the *revenant* quality, coming back painfully to haunt her. Bell's experience is of course prefigured in the novel, when Lily, painting her picture, has 'the old horror' ('to want and want and not to have' [TL, 186]) blotted out by the reappearance, 'quite simply', of Mrs Ramsay on the step. But for Lily this

reappearance of Mrs Ramsay is only one moment in the un-
folding drama of her sustained contemplation of Mrs Ramsay's beauty. It testifies to the strength and significance of the
visual attention which Lily has been giving her.

But Bell is taken quite by surprise. Her excitement at 'meeting [her mother] again' ('for the last two days I have hardly
been able to attend to daily life' [L, III, 11 May 1927, 572])
means that she is 'more incapable than anyone else in the
world of making an aesthetic judgement on it' (L, III, 11 May
1927, 572). But Woolf's reply suggests that it was not necessarily an aesthetic judgement that she wanted. 'No letter
pleased me one tenth as much as yours did . . . . I'm in a
terrible state of pleasure that you should think Mrs Ramsay
so like mother' (L, III, 25 May 1927, 383). The 'terrible . . .
pleasure', which is in a sense the theme of the novel, is partly
the risk of bringing her parents into her fictional world.
Woolf, like Lily, was calling up her ghosts. When Lily's finally
materialise they have lost the power to harm: 'Mrs Ramsay –
it was part of her perfect goodness to Lily – sat there quite
simply, in the chair, flicked her needles to and fro, knitted her
reddish-brown stocking, cast her shadow on the step. There
she sat' (TL, 186). It is with the same sudden and unexpected
immediacy that Woolf's lips start 'syllabling of their own
accord'. For both Lily and Woolf the body – the eyes, the
mouth – has taken over and started hallucinating its own
reality. Mrs Ramsay appears like an epiphany: 'there she sat'
(TL, 186).

It is through the use of such phrases – almost mnemonics –
that we can appreciate the closeness in Woolf's mind of her
mother and Mrs Ramsay. 'Certainly there she was', wrote
Woolf almost forty-five years after the death of her mother,
Julia Stephen. 'There she was, in the very centre of that great
Cathedral space which was childhood' (SP, 94). Lily, in the
silence of Mrs Ramsay's gazing out to sea, uses similar words:
she 'felt as if a door had been opened, and one went in and
stood gazing silently about in a high cathedral-like place, very
dark, very solemn' (TL, 159). Both Julia Stephen and Mrs

Ramsay have the ability to make sense of space, to order the chaos of life and human impressions into a harmonious repose. Both are described as 'upright' (R, 42; TL, 181); both are frenziedly active ('someone was always interrupting' the child Virginia's time with her mother [SP, 97]; Mrs Ramsay never lies 'reading, a whole morning on the lawn' [TL, 180]); and both have a Greek beauty (R, 49; TL, 32). Mrs Ramsay sends Cam to sleep by murmuring about 'valleys and flowers and bells ringing and birds singing and little goats and antelopes' (TL, 106). Julia Stephen used to come up to see that the children were asleep and soothe them by telling them to 'think of all the lovely things [they] could imagine. Rainbows and bells . . .' (SP, 95). And both are astonishingly beautiful.

Another construction in the novel to have the quality of the mnemonic is the superlative. But the superlative is a revelation as well as a mnemonic. Charles Tansley, watching Mrs Ramsay pause for a moment in front of a picture of Queen Victoria, suddenly realises 'that it was this: it was this: – she was the most beautiful person he had ever seen' (TL, 18). Virginia Woolf wrote of her mother that she was 'the most beautiful of women' (R, 36). It was Leslie Stephen, Woolf's father, who coined the phrase originally: 'she was the most beautiful woman I ever saw'.[5] Woolf wrote that she deliberately refrained from re-reading her father's letters or his *Mausoleum Book*, a life of her mother, before writing her novel. However, some phrases and the tone of worship in which they are written must have blended with her own memory, so that her recollections of her mother are not only of a person, but of phrases, descriptions, myths. A mythical feminine beauty, associated with Julia Stephen, is installed in *To the Lighthouse* as the central focus of erotic and artistic attention. In spite of its exploration of Lily's ambivalence towards Mrs Ramsay, the novel still turns on the image of her beauty. It is an open question how far this prevents the novel from following through the implications of its own unease, its dissatisfaction with the kind of femininity that Mrs Ramsay sustains. For it is she for whom the novel yearns;

and it is hard, as readers, to resist her powers of seduction.

Woolf's recollections of her father are echoed in her descriptions of Mr Ramsay. 'We made him the type of all that we hated in our lives; he was the tyrant of inconceivable selfishness' writes Woolf of her father (R, 65). James and Cam, on their way to the boat, vow 'to stand by each other and carry out the great compact – to resist tyranny to the death' (TL, 152). Both pairs of children (Virginia and Vanessa, James and Cam) are oppressed by the rites of their fathers' grief, and Lily, like Vanessa Stephen, is forced to endure an exaggerated and embarrassing demand for feminine sympathy (SP, 146; TL, 142). Yet both Cam and Virginia remember a more benign paternal figure. The child Cam, 'watching her father as he wrote in his study, . . . thought (now sitting in the boat) he was most lovable, he was most wise; he was not vain nor a tyrant' (TL, 175). The child Virginia would go up to her father's study to fetch a new book: 'For some time we would talk and then, feeling soothed, stimulated, full of love for this unworldly, very distinguished, lonely man, I would go down to the drawing-room again' (SP, 158). In *To the Lighthouse* the benignity of Mr Ramsay the intellectual is complicated by his incessant demands for reassurance about the importance of his work (TL, 38–9). Leslie Stephen's letters to his wife show that this was a feature of his marriage as well: 'when I am by myself I always begin thinking what poor stuff all my writing is.'[6]

Woolf, like Lily, was painting portraits. Where Lily tries to bring different masses and colours into relation, Woolf arranges echoes, acoustic images, to produce recognisable pictures in words. 'Most beautiful' studs her non-fictional and fictional representations of her mother. Her mother and Mrs Ramsay are together set up as a limit which cannot be passed, or even reached. The portrait of Mrs Ramsay, for both Lily and Woolf, lies at the edge of what is possible. She is the bourn of memory, of imagination: she is their horizon. For this reason Woolf is confused at what may have gone into this most intense of creations.

I'm in a terrible state of pleasure that you should think Mrs
Ramsay so like mother. At the same time, it is a psychological
mystery why she should be: how a child could know about her;
except that she has always haunted me, partly, I suppose, her
beauty; and then dying at that moment, I suppose she cut a
great figure on one's mind when it was just awake, and had not
any experience of life – Only then one would have suspected
that one had made up a sham – an ideal. Probably there is a
great deal of you in Mrs Ramsay; though, in fact, I think you
and mother are very different in my mind. (Virginia Woolf to
Vanessa Bell, L, III, 25 May 1927, 383)

Julia Stephen's dying at the moment when Virginia was
entering puberty (she was 13) cast her as a symbol of the lost
innocence and idyll of childhood, and made maturity and
maternity seem difficult and irrevocably lost to the young
Virginia, who suffered torments of self-consciousness all her
life. The 'sham' that Woolf suspects in her novel is her failure
to conceive of her mother as other than a limit, a superlative.
Her other model of maternity, her sister, only confirmed
motherhood as the distant horizon on which femininity was
finally resolved. 'I always measure myself against her', wrote
Woolf at the end of 1927, '& find her much the largest, most
humane of the two of us . . . as she [battles?] her way so
nonchalantly modestly, almost anonymously past the goal,
with her children round her' (D, III, 22 December 1927, 168).
Vanessa Bell, as much as Julia Stephen, had come to express
maternity in Woolf's life, such that Woolf presumes that, as she
thought of her mother and her relation to her children, 'something of Nessa leaked in' (Virginia Woolf to Roger Fry, L, III,
27 May 1927, 386). Certainly the feeling of life as something
to be battled against is associated by Woolf not so much with
Julia Stephen (who 'had inborn in her and [had] acquired a
deep sense of the futility of all effort, the mystery of life' [R,
41]) as with Mrs Ramsay (TL, 58) and with Virginia and
Vanessa: 'how proud I am of her [Vanessa's] triumphant
winning of all our battles' (D, III, 22 December 1927, 168).

Mrs Ramsay, then, is not simply Julia Stephen. She has
many of the qualities Woolf associated with Vanessa Bell's

motherhood. But the strain of missing her ('to want and not to have – to want and want – how that wrung the heart, and wrung it again and again!' [TL, 165]) is associated not with Vanessa Bell, and not even, in the autobiographical texts, with Julia Stephen. It was Vita Sackville-West, Virginia's new friend and lover, whom she was missing in the early months of 1926 when she was writing *To the Lighthouse*. Woolf wrote to Sackville-West in Teheran, where Sackville-West was visiting her diplomat husband: 'oh but there's Vita too – thats [*sic*] not a pigmy egotism – wanting her' (L, III, 31 January 1926, 237). In her diary for 23 February 1926, she writes in the same entry of the 'fertility & fluency' with which she is writing her novel, and of her longing for Sackville-West.

> Vita is a dumb letter writer, & I miss her. I miss the glow & the flattery & the festival. I miss her, I suppose, not very intimately. Nevertheless, I do miss her, & wish it were May 10th [the date of Sackville-West's return]; & then I don't wish it; for I have such a razor edge to my palette that seeing people often disgusts me of seeing them. (D, III, 23 February 1926, 59)

Woolf's phrases and images for the loss of Sackville-West appear in the novel as expressions of grief for Mrs Ramsay. Lily's missing of Mrs Ramsay is similarly unintimate (earlier in the book she has laughed to think how little Mrs Ramsay understands her), and similarly vacillatory. She does not miss her at all 'among the coffee cups at breakfast' (TL, 168), and then suddenly 'a hot liquid' rolls down her cheeks (TL, 166). The 'razor edge to my palette' (note Woolf's slip in the diary entry of 'palette' – the object with which Lily is busy – for 'palate') becomes, in *To the Lighthouse*: 'for whatever reason [Lily] could not achieve that razor edge of balance between two opposite forces' (TL, 178). To miss Sackville-West, who 'lavishes on me the maternal protection which, for some reason, is what I have always most wished from everyone' (D, III, 21 December 1925, 52), is to experience the strain of the withdrawal of maternal presence. As Woolf feels the strain, she finds phrases that will define the rhythm of Lily's grief for Mrs Ramsay.

Woolf was repeatedly interrupted as she worked to finish *To the Lighthouse*. Not by emotions, like her longing for Sackville-West – those, as we have seen, she would weave into the texture of *To the Lighthouse*. But her body several times let her down. Having begun to write on 6 August 1925, she would be forced to break off two weeks later.

> Fell down in a faint at Charleston, in the middle of Q.'s [her nephew Quentin Bell's] birthday party: & then have lain about here, in that odd amphibious life of headache, for a fortnight. This has rammed a big hole in my 8 weeks which were to be stuffed so full. (D, III, 5 September 1925, 38–9)

Holes are rammed in *To the Lighthouse* too: the hole of the middle section, the gap of Mrs Ramsay's death. Yet, having recovered to a certain extent her equilibrium, Woolf is still satisfied with the start she has made. 'I have made a very quick & flourishing attack on To the Lighthouse, all the same – 22 pages straight off in less than a fortnight' (D, III, 5 September 1925, 39). She imagines herself riding and determined to subdue that intractable beast, life: 'never be unseated by the shying of that undependable brute, life, hag ridden as she is by my own queer, difficult nervous system' (D, III, 5 September 1925, 39). Mrs Ramsay is aware of a similar enemy, although she imagines hers to be not internal but external: 'she felt this thing that she called life terrible, hostile, and quick to pounce on you if you gave it a chance. There were the eternal problems: suffering; death; the poor' (TL, 58). Both women live in danger. For Mrs Ramsay the symbol of that danger is the lighthouse, repeatedly warning against an invisible peril. But both are also dangerous themselves. It is Woolf's own body – her femaleness – which she must constantly fend off; Mrs Ramsay, associated as she is with the domestic stability of the house and the island, is the obstacle that the ships must avoid. We shall see that her presence has an almost siren-like effect on passing men.

Land and sea, in Woolf's novel and in her mental life, are in constant battle. The day she finished *To the Lighthouse*, Woolf passed an agonised night.

Woke up perhaps at 3. Oh its beginning its coming – the horror – physically like a painful wave swelling about the heart – tossing me up. I'm unhappy unhappy! Down – God, I wish I were dead. Pause. But why am I feeling this? Let me watch the wave rise. I watch. Vanessa. Children. Failure. Yes; I detect that. Failure failure. (The wave rises). Oh they laughed at my taste in green paint! Wave crashes. I wish I were dead! I've only a few more years to live I hope. I cant [*sic*] face this horror any more – (this is the wave spreading out over me). (D, III, 15 September 1926, 110)

In the silence of a completed manuscript, Woolf feels that she is drowning. Mrs Ramsay, hearing the waves 'like a ghostly roll of drums remorselessly beat the measure of life', also thinks of 'the destruction of the island and its engulfment in the sea' (TL, 20). The ultimate fear is of the erasure, the suffocation, of human identity (as happens in 'Time Passes').

Phyllis Rose, one of Woolf's biographers, suggests that Woolf felt this acute anxiety at the end of every book because to write was to mark herself out as different from her mother and, since everyone loved her mother, as essentially unlovable.[7] It is an acute moment of the self-consciousness Woolf always felt. Lily has something of the same feeling, aware of Mrs Ramsay presiding over the house full of sleeping children: 'Oh but, Lily would say, there was her father; her home; even, had she dared to say it, her painting. But all this seemed so little, so virginal, against the other' (TL, 49). Lily's doubt is over whether or not a childless woman is fully realised. The smallness that Lily feels about her life and her body is echoed in the indifference with which the wave of Woolf's despair crashes down on Woolf's negligible body, that body which is simultaneously a let-down and a threat. It is this strange tension – the failure of Mrs Ramsay's maternity to deliver the reassurance that it seems to promise – that the novel will explore.

2

Perspectives

To the Lighthouse opens with an answer: ' "Yes, of course, if it's fine tomorrow," said Mrs Ramsay. "But you'll have to be up with the lark," she added' (TL, 9). It is as though the reader, actualising Woolf's idea for her short story, interrupts. The rhythm established is simultaneously one of question and response, and of hiatus. Moreover, Mrs Ramsay's words counteract the effect of her opening affirmation. As she grants the unheard request, she introduces the notion of unpredictability and contingency: 'if', 'but'. She promises while admitting that in fact she can promise nothing. The narrative strategies of the novel, which we shall investigate in this chapter, are an attempt to negotiate this contradiction: to achieve climax without conclusion.

Mrs Ramsay and her youngest child James are sitting in the window of the drawing-room in early evening. Their conversation about going to the lighthouse is constantly interrupted in various ways. Typographically each sentence of the dialogue is followed by a substantial paragraph sometimes of silent reflections, sometimes of memories. These paragraphs are themselves cut short by another line from the dialogue, often a line of contradiction. ' "But,' said his father, stopping in front of the drawing-room window, "it won't be fine". . . . "Nonsense," said Mrs Ramsay, with great severity' (TL, 9; 11). The opening of the novel has a conflictual rhythm which draws on the contradiction of Mrs Ramsay's promise at the beginning.

The spoken words punctuate a silent world of thought and memory which sometimes lasts for the amount of time which passes in the novel between each line of dialogue, and sometimes seems to extend far beyond it. Mrs Ramsay has an image for this misfit between public and private time:

> When life sank down for a moment, the range of experience seemed limitless. And to everybody there was always this sense of unlimited resources, she supposed; one after another, she, Lily, Augustus Carmichael, must feel, our apparitions, the things you know us by, are simply childish. Beneath it is all dark, it is all spreading, it is unfathomably deep; but now and again we rise to the surface and that is what you see us by. Her horizon seemed to her limitless. (TL, 60)

Mrs Ramsay would like to think that the things by which we are known – our words, our deeds, the dialogue which forms the skeleton of the first sections of the novel – are superficial, like the waves which ruffle the surface of the sea. The real horizon that the family and guests see as they gaze from the window of the house marks the limit of vision; the underwater horizon – the darkness in which Mrs Ramsay moves – is an expression of infinity, an invitation to range without stall or check. 'This core of darkness could go anywhere, for no one saw it' (TL, 61).

But the absolute freedom which Mrs Ramsay thinks she has places limits on relationships – *is* in fact their limit. Mr Ramsay, passing, is saddened by 'the sternness at the heart of her beauty' (TL, 62). Later, on their walk: 'he did not like to see her look so sad, he said. Only wool gathering, she protested, flushing a little. They both felt uncomfortable, as if they did not know whether to go on or go back' (TL, 65). Her flush is a signal that a boundary has been reached; her silence is a sign of resistance. 'No, they could not share that; they could not say that' (TL, 65). As their conversation stalls, they arrive at the gap in the hedge, 'and there was the Lighthouse again' (TL, 65), symbol of danger, of trespass; agent of interruption, of exposure. Mrs Ramsay, annoyed ('she disliked anything that reminded her that she had been seen sitting thinking'

[TL, 65]) will not look at it. It is a reminder of what she must fight against: that Mr Ramsay seeks to pass the limit of human relations which the lighthouse marks, the line between the liminal zone of the waves and the darkness of the deep and private ocean.

It is not only the lighthouse which marks limits. The movement of the narrative perspective that Auerbach charts in 'The Brown Stocking' (a chapter in his classic *Mimesis*, 1946) is also one of definition of limit. Auerbach's passage covers Section 5 of Part I (pp. 29–32). The progress of the dialogue, as we have seen, is constantly retarded by the intrusion of long silent passages of memory or reflection; and private thought is also hemmed in by the intermittent sentences of dialogue. The spoken words in their inverted commas break into the solid paragraphs of reflection which surround them, like markers; like the lighthouse or, as Mr Ramsay imagines himself, like 'a stake driven into the bed of a channel upon which the gulls perch and the waves beat . . . marking the channel out there in the floods alone' (TL, 45). The inverted commas stake out the spreading waters of private thought.

Mrs Ramsay's words – both the words she speaks and the words she thinks – are punctuated in various different ways. After her first sentence (in Auerbach's extract), we hear her thoughts as a form of indirect speech, introduced by 'that': 'thinking that Lily's charm was her Chinese eyes' (TL, 29). In the second paragraph the dashes ('– William and Lily should marry –') indicate the reproduction of Mrs Ramsay's tone and words (in direct speech it might have been written: ' "William and Lily should marry!" '). Her words are reported rather than transcribed, although without the signal 'that' which introduced indirect thought earlier. This means that the narrative can slide in and out of her mind, speaking sometimes with her voice, sometimes reporting her thoughts, and sometimes as an omniscient narrator observing the scene ('raising her eyes to glance at William Bankes and Lily Briscoe' [TL, 29]). The impression given is one of fluidity, of a multiplicity of possible perspectives and tones all existing simultaneously and held in suspension by the turns of the narrative. As soon as one train of thought reaches resolution, or faces some kind of check, the narrative simply flows easily into another. This produces a peculiar feeling of simultaneous peace and restlessness. Sentences are never actually prevented from continuing, but lines of thought are perpetually taken up only to be dropped. This means that resolutions are only ever local, and the project of the novel is to find a way of combining its characteristic fluidity with the achievement of finality. Although Woolf seems to have found multiple viewpoints congenial, the discontent of an unsettled narrative is perhaps responsible for the novel's strange obsession with solutions. We shall look more closely at this, in connection with Mrs Ramsay, in the next chapter.

Whatever its difficulties, it was this adaptability – this chameleon-like quality – of the narrative voice that was Virginia Woolf's major innovation in this novel. In a famous statement of her purpose, she wrote that:

> Life is not a series of gig-lamps symmetrically arranged; life is a luminous halo, a semi-transparent envelope surrounding us from the beginning of consciousness to the end. Is it not the task of the novelist to convey this varying, this unknown and uncircumscribed spirit, whatever aberration or complexity it may display, with as little mixture of the alien and external as possible?[1]

Here the object of the novelist's attention is a light, a 'halo' which acts as a filter for our perceptions of the world. Lily has a rather different image:

> Only like a bee, drawn by some sweetness or sharpness in the air intangible to touch or taste, one haunted the dome-shaped hive, ranged the wastes of the air over the countries of the world alone, and then haunted the hives with their murmurs and their stirrings; the hives which were people. (TL, 51)

In this case the image for the artistic object is one of sound ('stirrings') and also of 'sweetness'. The compulsion and pleasure that Lily feels in pondering the characters of others is emphasised, along with her homing instinct.

It is fascination with Mrs Ramsay that has prompted Lily's thoughts on the limits to human intimacy, and it is with Mrs Ramsay that her conclusions come to be associated:

> for days there hung about [Mrs Ramsay], as after a dream some subtle change is felt in the person one has dreamt of, more vividly than anything she said, the sound of murmuring and, as she sat in the wicker arm-chair in the drawing-room window she wore, to Lily's eyes, an august shape; the shape of a dome. (TL, 51)

Lily's questions about love and knowledge come back to rest where they started, with Mrs Ramsay 'in the wicker arm-chair in the drawing-room window' (TL, 51). Repeatedly, the image of Mrs Ramsay will come to stand for the closure for which the novel so longs. In bringing the wandering Lily back home, Mrs Ramsay promises that somewhere in the world there is still the possibility of belonging. But, as we saw, we must be suspicious of Mrs Ramsay's promises, and suspicious, too, of the novel's investment in her.

Auerbach describes the shape of the narrative in Section 5 as follows:

> This entirely insignificant occurrence [the measuring of the stocking] is constantly interspersed with other elements which, although they do not interrupt its progress, take up far more time in the narration than the whole scene can possibly have lasted. Most of these elements are inner processes, that is, movements within the consciousness of individual personages, and not necessarily of personages involved in the exterior occurrence but also of others who are not even present at the time: 'people', or 'Mr. Bankes'. In addition other exterior occurrences which might be called secondary and which pertain to quite different times and places (the telephone conversation, the construction of the building, for example) are worked in and made to serve as the frame for what goes on in the consciousness of third persons. (M, 529)

Auerbach stresses the elasticity of the narrative, which expands and contracts to accommodate not only 'inner processes' but also the perspectives of characters who are not even in the central scene of the extract: Bankes in London, for example. The narrative has a double flexibility. It operates in several time dimensions simultaneously (the moment in the window, the unspecified time of rumour, the day of Bankes' phone call), and ranges easily in space, sometimes calling on Mrs Ramsay in the Hebrides, and sometimes on Mr Bankes, at some previous time, in London. Auerbach refers to these shifts in perspective – both temporal and geographical – as interruptions which are nevertheless 'worked in' to the main narrative. Although the novel is full of people breaking into each other's train of thought, or suddenly crossing each other's line of vision, the function of the narrative is the continual transformation of interruption into new direction. Mrs Ramsay's knitting is a significant image of the working-in of different threads. The sight of William and Lily is a signal for Mrs Ramsay to think about their possible marriage: marriage, another knitting-together of lives.

The other image that Auerbach uses for this process of the transformation of interruption is that of the picture. Mr Bankes, replacing the receiver after his phone call to Mrs Ramsay, crosses the room 'to see what progress the workmen [are] making with an hotel which they were building at the back of his house' (TL, 32). As he muses on Mrs Ramsay, he thinks that 'if it was her beauty merely that one thought of, one must remember the quivering thing, the living thing (they were carrying bricks up a little plank as he watched them), and work it into the picture' (TL, 32). The novel itself 'works' the details at which Bankes is gazing into the movements of his thoughts. He looks through a window and sees Mrs Ramsay ('she clapped a deer-stalker's hat on her head; she ran across the lawn in goloshes to snatch a child from mischief' [TL, 32]), but behind that recollected image is the continued movement of workmen up a plank, like 'the quivering thing, the living thing' of which he thinks when he remembers Mrs Ramsay. The parenthesis interrupts and vitalises his thoughts by giving them a context, but also moves them on further by producing a feeling of double vision, Bankes seeing at once the workmen and the woman about whom he thinks.

In addition, parentheses remind us of the danger in which Bankes and the other characters live. The workmen walking the plank will be recalled later in Lily's image for beginning a picture: 'it was an odd road to be walking, this of painting. Out and out one went, further and further, until at last one seemed to be on a narrow plank, perfectly alone, over the sea' (TL, 160). The risk that both Bankes and Lily take is that of painting Mrs Ramsay. Both look through a window and focus on her. Both wonder what to include. 'Some freak of idiosyncrasy', thinks Mr Bankes, and finally cannot decide: 'he did not know. He did not know. He must go to his work' (TL, 32). Lily's risk is much more immediate, for she exposes herself to grief, to loss, by thinking of Mrs Ramsay after her demise. The marginal threat of the workmen walking the plank has become the ever-present reality of Mrs Ramsay's death: 'no one had seen her step off her strip of board into the waters of annihilation' (TL, 167).

Auerbach points out that the theme of the passage he chooses to comment on in his book is 'the solution of the enigma Mrs Ramsay' (M, 539). The connection between the different sections of this passage is that they are all 'looking at Mrs Ramsay' (M, 539), such that she shifts from being the subject of the gaze – the person whose words and whose thoughts are reported, from whose perspective the room is seen (as she measures the stocking she looks around at the furniture) – to being the gaze's object, a riddle whose solution promises understanding not only of the object of attention but of the self.

> However insignificant as an exterior event the framing occurrence (the measuring of the stocking) may be, the picture of Mrs Ramsay's face which arises from it remains present throughout the excursus; the excursus itself is nothing but a background for that picture, which seems as it were to open into the depths of time – just as the first excursus, released by Mrs Ramsay's unintentional glance at the furniture, was an opening of the picture into the depths of consciousness. (M, 540)

Pictures of Mrs Ramsay are never two-dimensional. The

open windows to which she attaches so much importance ('windows should be open, and doors shut' [TL, 30]) give onto distant horizons of private thought and vanishing time. The third dimension comes in many forms: her own thoughts; the thoughts of others; another time; another place. People's lives recede before them as they turn, in desire for Mrs Ramsay, for one last look. The movement of their bodies is inhibited – the closed door – but the movement of the mind and the vision is not. As Mrs Ramsay thinks, 'it is all dark, it is all spreading, it is unfathomably deep' (TL, 60) – both a sensation and a perspective.

The 'excursus' to which Auerbach refers, opening 'into the depths of time', is the passage signalled by Mrs Ramsay's discovery that the stocking is too short. The passage is a series of questions (we remember again how often Mrs Ramsay is also associated with answers).

> Never did anybody look so sad. Bitter and black, half-way down, in the darkness, in the shaft which ran from the sunlight to the depths, perhaps a tear formed; a tear fell; the waters swayed this way and that, received it, and were at rest. Never did anybody look so sad.
> But was it nothing but looks? people said. What was there behind it – her beauty, her splendour? Had he blown his brains out, they asked, had he died the week before they were married – some other, earlier lover, of whom rumours reached one? Or was there nothing? nothing but an incomparable beauty which she lived behind, and could do nothing to disturb? (TL, 31)

The tone of the passage is one of doubt. The feeling expressed is similar to that which the child Virginia reported when looking at her mother reading:

> Struck by the gravity of her face, [I] told myself that her first husband had been a clergyman and that she was thinking, as she read what he had read, of him. This was a fable on my part; but it shows that she looked very sad when she was not talking. (SP, 96)

The beauty of both Julia Stephen and Mrs Ramsay seems to be troubling as well as arresting. Originally, in her draft of *To the Lighthouse* Woolf wrote: 'there had been something', suggesting that there was a reason for Mrs Ramsay's sadness, but then she crossed it out.[2] The question ('but was it nothing but looks?') in the final version is less a concrete inquiry about Mrs Ramsay's past, and more the expression of some irresolution at the heart of her beauty. She is at once question and answer, but in being both at once, she can be neither with any conviction. It is this lack of conviction which produces the insistence on her image as both a demand and a gift. This contradiction will be explored more fully in the chapters that follow.

It is not only Mrs Ramsay who is an uncertainty here, however. Auerbach has a few more questions to ask of the novel at this point: 'Who is speaking in this paragraph? Who is looking at Mrs Ramsay here, who concludes that never did anybody look so sad?' (M, 531). There is no one else in the room. William and Lily have walked past; James is busy fidgeting. Auerbach is forced to conclude that the perspective in this paragraph is the author's, 'but she does not seem to bear in mind that she is the author and hence ought to know how matters stand with her characters' (M, 531). A deliberate myopia is assumed (Mrs Ramsay is also short-sighted [TL, 68]) so that an impression of doubt and ignorance is set up. We are deprived of a perspective we have come to expect in the novel: the perspective of the narrator who has access to characters' histories, thoughts and feelings. Instead, although we have many different points of view in the novel (and this was a technique that has also been used by Henry James), all perspectives have their own limits. There is an implicit question in almost all the perspectives represented here, the question that Lily poses early in the novel: 'How did one judge people, think of them? How did one add up this and that and conclude that it was liking one felt, or disliking? And to those words, what meaning attached, after all?' (TL, 27).

The doubt with which almost every perspective is endowed – its myopia – is an expression of a more profound doubt about human relations. It is not even an uncertainty about whether or not we know other people; it is a radical disquiet about the terms on which it is possible to relate to them. Dispute about the gaze – how clearly and from what angle we see someone or something – is also dispute about the emotional ordering of our lives. Mrs Ramsay keeps wondering: 'for her own self-satisfaction was it that she wished so instinctively to help, to give, that people might say of her, "O Mrs Ramsay! dear Mrs Ramsay! . . . Mrs Ramsay, of course!" and need her and send for her and admire her?' (TL, 42). As she tries to expose herself to the searchlight of moral analysis, Mrs Ramsay questions her impulse 'to help, to give' as an attempt to re-order relations so that she is the universal object of admiration – the object of the gaze. The speaking of her name – ' "O Mrs Ramsay!" ' – is a tribute to her in the same way that Tansley's breathless stare (TL, 18) and Bankes' rapturous contemplation (TL, 48) make her the focal point of their own private pictures. The shifting perspectives in the novel are not merely a trick of symbolic method: they are attempts to dramatise profound and only half-expressed questions about vision, power and love. The fact that it is Mrs Ramsay who is so often a focal point is a signal that gender is an inextricable part of these questions.

Woolf was concerned that in the novel we should feel that we see more than one thing at once. We have already noted that this desire was particularly pronounced in the case of the ending of the novel. Woolf wonders 'how to bring Lily & Mrs R[amsay] together & make a combination of interest at the end . . . Could I do it in a parenthesis? so that one had the sense of reading the two things at the same time?' (D, III, 5 September 1926, 106). Parenthesis as a signal of simultaneity is a central feature of the novel's prose style, and not only at the end. We have already seen it used in the middle of Mr Bankes' reverie as he looks out of the window ('one must remember the quivering thing, the living thing (they were carrying bricks up a little plank as he watched them), and work it into the picture' [TL, 32]). Brackets also surround the whole passage about Bankes in London, so that it is 'framed', as Auerbach would say, not only by the sudden detail about the events occurring behind his house, but also, typographically, by the brackets themselves (Woolf was herself a printer and acutely aware of the appearance of text). Like the lighthouse, the brackets mark a boundary, introduce a change of scene and close it off again at the end. Within the brackets a distinct little narrative emerges.

Parentheses can be at once signals of simultaneity and of digression. Like all digressions in this novel, sentences in brackets are swept along in the current of the narrative. Woolf wrote in her preliminary notes for the draft: 'my aim being to find a unit ~~wh~~ for the sentence which shall be less emphatic & intense than that in Mrs. D[alloway]: an everyday sentence for carrying on the narrative easily.'[3] 'Carrying on' and 'work[ing] . . . in' are apparently phrases for the same preoccupation. Pictures frame pictures in a series receding to infinity. Mr Bankes in London is an unexpected insertion into a lengthy description of Mrs Ramsay in the window, but Bankes also contributes to that description. As he looks out of his own window, he looks into his past, superimposing Mrs Ramsay in her goloshes on the intrepid plank-walking workmen. As readers, we too look into the window of the brackets and see an episode which occurred prior to the main action of the scene. The vanishing point of our vision, and of Mr Bankes', is, as usual, Mrs Ramsay.

Parentheses, then, initiate multiple regressions. But they can also be little asides, explanations, pointers to what is going on. Lily in this passage is thinking about Mr Bankes.

> I respect you (she addressed him silently) in every atom; you are not vain; you are entirely impersonal; you are finer than Mr Ramsay; you are the finest human being that I know; you have neither wife nor child (without any sexual feeling, she longed to cherish that loneliness), you live for science (involuntarily, sections of potatoes rose before her eyes); praise would be an insult to you; generous, pure-hearted, heroic man! (TL, 27)

Here the parentheses signal sudden and momentary switches in perspective. The rhythm that is set up is almost dialogic:

the question and answer model which we have come to see is central to the structure and themes of the novel. The narrative is thrown backwards and forwards between Lily's voice, with its intonation mimicked exactly, even though we know she is not speaking these words, and a commentary which seems to respond to her silent thoughts. Lily's dwelling on the austerity of Bankes' life indicates not only Bankes' desire for solitude, but also her own – and at the same time shows her resistance to her own loneliness. She wants at once to extend and to limit, to see more of Bankes and less of herself. This conflict is represented in the simultaneous development of two registers: the succession of main clauses inscribing Lily's voice, and the little interruptions of the parentheses, at the corner of Lily's eye. The final set of brackets describes a sudden obstruction of her vision: the rising of potatoes before her eyes. Yet this obstruction too is part of the movement of her thought: it is her habit to conceptualise intellectual disciplines as material objects ('she always saw, when she thought of Mr Ramsay's work, a scrubbed kitchen table' [TL, 26]).

The most famous parentheses of *To the Lighthouse* occur in the middle section. Events that would seem to deserve a place at the centre of the action – the death of Mrs Ramsay, for example – take place in brackets and are apparently marginal to the main preoccupations of the narrative, these being the gradual change in the fabric of the island and of the house. '[Mr Ramsay stumbling along a passage stretched his arms out one dark morning, but, Mrs Ramsay having died rather suddenly the night before, he stretched his arms out. They remained empty]' (TL, 120). (The slight confusion here and the repetition of 'he stretched his arms out' are apparently publishing errors. Woolf corrected the proofs prepared by the Hogarth Press and sent them to the United States, where they were used as setting copy for the simultaneous American edition by Harcourt Brace.[4] The American edition of this passage reads, more sensibly: '[Mr. Ramsay, stumbling along a passage one dark morning, stretched his arms out, but Mrs. Ramsay having died rather suddenly the night before, his arms, though stretched out, remained empty.]'⁵)

The discontinuity marked by the square brackets is a symptom of the radical discontinuity caused by the event recounted within the brackets: the death of Mrs Ramsay and the fundamental re-ordering of relations that that loss will demand. Yet the brackets also signal a focal point. Looking into the creaking house we see into the heart of it and are presented with the dying Mrs Ramsay. The house in its slow decay seems to be indifferent to the fate of its displaced inhabitants (we remember this function of brackets – to shift location – from the Bankes episode earlier in the novel). Whilst Mr Bankes and the 'people' ('But was it nothing but looks? people said.' [TL, 31]) both directed their attention towards Mrs Ramsay, she was easily identified as the common object of their gazes; but to look into the house and see her even there is a shock. The square brackets signal the violence with which we are forced to associate the decay of the house with that of Mrs Ramsay, and to admit that wherever we look, she is in the end what we see. The brackets indicate at once a break in the narrative, and its essential truth.

This change in the tone of the parentheses will last until the end of the novel. Square brackets, never used in the first part, intrude continually in the final part, 'The Lighthouse'. John Mepham has compared the function of round and square brackets in the novel as analogous to the distinction between metonym and metaphor. Metonym involves a chain of associations, one thing leading to another; metaphor is the identity or fusion of two entities previously thought to be separate.

> Whereas in Part I we find metonymic transitions and the narration of non-simultaneous but causally related events in round brackets, in Part III [and Part II] we find metaphoric relations established by the narration of simultaneous but non-related events between square brackets.⁶

The metaphoric relation of which Mepham writes is exactly the sense at which Woolf was aiming, that 'of reading the two things at the same time' (D, III, 5 September 1926, 106). It is both the shock of death, and the shock of recognition.

It is clear, therefore, that the novel is obsessed with Mrs Ramsay. Although it has sometimes been seen as a novel that criticises the roles assigned to husband and wife in traditional marriage, it is itself guilty of setting up a very traditional feminine beauty (Mrs Ramsay's) as a potential answer to any problem. Woolf appears to feel nostalgic for, as well as critical of, the ideal of Victorian womanhood. Thus Mrs Ramsay, while she seems to open up questions and perspectives, also succeeds in closing them. Wherever the characters look, Mrs Ramsay blocks their view. Any sustained criticism in the novel of gender roles is brought up short by its investment in the beauty of the maternal woman. The line which Lily draws through her painting could be simply an expression of frustration, the novel's way of giving up on the problem of simultaneously challenging and adoring Mrs Ramsay. For the scene on which the novel closes is precisely the scene on which it opened: Mrs Ramsay and James in the window.

3

Reading Aloud

While she was writing *To the Lighthouse*, Virginia Woolf wrote in her diary: 'I think I will find some theory about fiction . . . the one I have in view, is about *perspective*' (D, III, 7 December 1925, 50). The novel, dominated as it is by Lily's difficulties with looking, and her attempts to organise the perspectives of her painting, goes some way towards finding a practice, if not a theory, of perspective in fiction. The construction of the spectating subject has been extensively theorised by critics of film. In this chapter I will suggest that, simultaneously with the expansion of the film industry, Woolf was drawing her own conclusions about the function of the look in the world of art. Her ideas about focal points and perspectives are worked, in literary form, into a politics of gender relations. The representation of Mrs Ramsay's beauty becomes a challenge and a fetish in *To the Lighthouse*, much as the production of Hollywood film stars had been in the early years of cinema.

To the Lighthouse proceeds from scene to scene. For the first twelve sections of the book, Mrs Ramsay and James are sitting still in the window of the house. At first she is knitting and he is cutting out pictures (the knitting symbolic of the weaving-in of straying narrative threads, and the cutting-out mimicking Lily's project as a painter). Other characters, by contrast, are continually in movement: Mr Ramsay and Tansley walk 'up and down, up and down the terrace' (TL, 11); Mr Ramsay blunders around reciting 'The Charge of the

Light Brigade' ('he would not stand still and look at her picture' [TL, 21]); Lily and Bankes stroll 'down the garden in the usual direction' (TL, 23); Carmichael goes shuffling past (TL, 41); and 'that wild villain, Cam, dashing past . . . would not stop for Mr Bankes and Lily Briscoe' (TL, 53). As Gillian Beer has commented, 'in the novel there is an extraordinary sense of the substantiality of people'.[1] Mrs Ramsay and James in the window are the still point of this world of movement and collision. The novel returns constantly to Mrs Ramsay's activities or to her perspective, as do the characters. To get their bearings, they turn towards the house and look at her. The nourishment they derive from such a gaze is on occasion almost physical: 'the sight of them [Mrs Ramsay and James] fortified [Mr Ramsay] and satisfied him and consecrated his effort' (TL, 35).

As she worked on *To the Lighthouse*, Woolf was also writing an occasional piece about looking, called 'The cinema' (1926). 'The cinema', like *To the Lighthouse*, is engaged in evolving an aesthetics of the gaze, and many of its insights are relevant to contemporary film theory. In the piece, Woolf makes three significant points. The first is to do with pleasure. She liked going to the cinema: 'the eye licks it all up instantaneously, and the brain, agreeably titillated, settles down to watch things happening without bestiring itself to think' (C, 268). The initial sensation of the film spectator, then, is one of unmediated visual pleasure.

But this immediacy is soon compromised. The brain must wake up. 'The eye is in difficulties. The eye wants help. The eye says to the brain, "Something is happening which I do not in the least understand. You are needeed" ' (C, 268). The cinematic image suddenly seems rather less present than it did

They [the images] have become not more beautiful in the sense in which pictures are beautiful, but shall we call it (our vocabulary is miserably insufficient) more real, or real with a different reality from that which we perceive in daily life? We behold them as they are when we are not there. We see life as it is when we have no part in it. (C, 269)

The spectator experiences the film as a dramatisation of his or her own absence. Although his or her look (and brain) control the cinematic scene by decoding it, interpreting the two-dimensional screen image as a three-dimensional world, the spectators themselves are radically excluded from the scene of the film. They cannot change it, they cannot enter it, and they cannot even end it.

This means that the experience of the film is at once one of immortality ('this beauty will continue, and this beauty will flourish whether we behold it or not' [C, 269]) and of ephemerality, absence ('we are beholding a world which has gone beneath the waves' [C, 269]). That immortality/ephemerality contradiction is really a crisis in the spectator. He or she is always implied by the film, seeing only what the camera allows. At the same time the individual spectator is a constant irrelevance. He or she could be anyone, could get up and leave the cinema, and the film would still continue. In that sense he or she is never entirely present, is always struggling with his or her own implied absence.

Woolf's third point is about the possibility of narrative transitions that are held out by the cinema.

> The past could be unrolled, distances annihilated, and the gulfs which dislocate novels (when, for instance, Tolstoy has to pass from Levin to Anna and in doing so jars his story and wrenches and arrests our sympathies) could by the sameness of the background, by the repetition of some scene, be smoothed away. (C, 272)

This is the kind of effortless transition which Woolf aimed at in the narrative shifts of *To the Lighthouse*, although there the strategy is more complicated than simply the sameness of the setting. As we have seen, she used a mixture of parenthesis and point of view to control what, in 'The cinema', she calls the 'violent changes of emotion produced by their [the emotions'] collision' (C, 272). The crisis of presence/absence experienced by the spectator is constantly postponed by a 'smoothing-away' of its effects in both cinematic and fictional narrative.

Repeated echoes of *To the Lighthouse* in 'The cinema' show that the two texts are part of the same project. 'We behold them as they are when we are not there' (C, 269) is heard again in Andrew's ' "Think of a kitchen table then," he told her, "when you're not there" ' (TL, 26). The story of *To the Lighthouse* lies behind Woolf's sentence in 'The cinema': 'the war sprung its chasm at the feet of all this innocence and ignorance' (C, 269). Most significantly, Woolf's definition of cinematic language ('some residue of visual emotion . . . something abstract, something which moves with controlled and conscious art' [C, 271]) is echoed in the language of female desire in *To the Lighthouse*. In 'The cinema' she poses the question: 'is there, we ask, some secret language which we feel and see, but never speak, and, if so, could this be made visible to the eye?' (C, 270–1). In *To the Lighthouse*, of Lily and Mrs Ramsay, she writes:

> She [Lily] imagined how in the chambers of the mind and heart of the woman who was, physically, touching her, were stood, like the treasures in the tombs of kings, tablets bearing sacred inscriptions, which if one could spell them out would teach one everything, but they would never be offered openly, never be made public. (TL, 50)

The shared imagery of these two works suggests that what Woolf was groping towards in these years was an aesthetics that would take account of gender and of perspective; of femininity and the look. It is as a part of this endeavour that *To the Lighthouse* should properly be viewed. The novel is a contribution to a debate which is still very much alive in film theory today: how to theorise woman as both object and subject of the look, and how to understand the construction of the subject as an effect of the object conceived to be looked at.

As Mary Ann Doane comments: 'historically, there has always been a certain imbrication of the cinematic image and the representation of the woman.'[2] The production of the Hollywood star is the most obvious example of this, but socially and culturally woman was there to be looked at long before Hollywood. Thorstein Veblen in *The Theory of the Leisure Class* (1899) had already noted that the function of middle- and upper-class wives was the '*conspicuous* [my italics] consumption of valuable goods' in order that their husbands' wealth should be displayed.[3] Woman as display is always related to man as proprietor: the adornment of women is a material sign that they are already claimed (the wedding ring is the simplest and most common example). Woman as spectacle – produced for consumption – often has a flavour of prohibition about her. Dressed to excite desire, her display of her husband's wealth must also act to limit desire's consequences, since it shows that she already belongs to one specific man.

Throughout the first ten sections of *To the Lighthouse* people keep looking at Mrs Ramsay. This shifting from position to position, people circling their objects, looking at them from all angles, is reproduced in the circulation of images through the text. The lighthouse, for example, appears now in association with one character (Mrs Ramsay 'flashing her needles, confident, upright . . . created drawing-room and kitchen, set them all aglow' [TL, 39]) and then with another (Mr Ramsay wishes he were one of those 'who, miraculously, lump all the letters together in one flash – the way of genius' [TL, 36]). The world of the novel is a series of perspectives, and of images, within whose order each character must find his or her own meaning, in relation to other members of the group, other ways of seeing things. The effect of these sections is kaleidoscopic, things momentarily falling into different patterns, different harmonies. The challenge for all the characters as they wander in the garden with their continual questions – ' "How then did it work out, all this?" ' (TL, 27) – is to come to rest, to find something recognisable and common to all the pictures: a solution. Mrs Ramsay seems to offer something close to this.

As we have seen, Mrs Ramsay's function in the narrative is very often contradictory: making promises she can't keep; offering both questions and answers. We saw at the end of

Chapter 2 that she blocks perspectives even as she opens them up. A classic article on women and cinema, 'Visual pleasure and narrative cinema' by Laura Mulvey, can offer us a vocabulary to understand Mrs Ramsay's appeal. Mulvey notes that images of women in films often impede the progress of cinematic narrative: 'the presence of woman is an indispensable element of spectacle in normal narrative film, yet her visual presence tends to work against the development of a story line, to freeze the flow of action in moments of erotic contemplation.'[4] The investment in the screen image of, say, Garbo, is so great that the camera sometimes pauses on her face for a considerable length of time – presumably to satisfy the drive that Mulvey believes is in part responsible for the pleasure of watching films: scopophilia, a pleasure in looking.[5] (Mulvey fails to deal adequately in this article with the problem of the gender of the spectator. This is a question we shall address later.)

But, according to Mulvey, woman's image can never be simply pleasurable: the 'female form . . . speaks castration and nothing else'; woman 'can exist only in relation to castration and cannot transcend it'.[6] Mulvey, drawing on Freud, assumes that the spectacle of the female body is always a threat to the male ego, which is always ready to succumb to castration anxiety, the fear of losing the penis. 'The woman as icon, displayed for the gaze and enjoyment of men, the active controllers of the look, always threatens to evoke the anxiety it originally signified.'[7] The response of the unspecified 'people' to Mrs Ramsay which asked 'but was it nothing but looks?' (TL, 31) demonstrates just such an unease.

That interrogatory reaction also exemplifies one of the two possible responses outlined by Mulvey to the fear evoked by the spectacle of the 'castrated' woman. The first, sadistic response is only intelligible within the Freudian scenario in which children first learn about sexual difference through their dramatic discovery, on seeing their mother's genitals for the first time, that women do not have penises. The sadistic response involves 'preoccupation with the re-enactment of the original trauma (investigating the woman, demystifying her mystery), counterbalanced by the devaluation, punishment or saving of the guilty object.'[8] The woman is blamed for her own lack of a penis, and consequently for the possible threat to the man's. It is important to remember that Ramsay, Tansley and Bankes all experience moments of enmity towards Mrs Ramsay, as well as moments of ecstatic admiration (but what they admire, it is worth noting, is always simply her beauty, her surface).

This admiration is covered by Mulvey's description of the second possible response to woman as icon. This relies on Freud's account of the aetiology, or causes, of fetishism (defined by Freud as the replacement of 'the normal sexual object . . . by another which bears some relation to it, but is entirely unsuited to serve the normal sexual aim' – for instance, hair, feet, underclothes).[9] The adoption of a fetish arises from the desire to repress the memory of the first sight of the 'castrated' female body. 'The fetish is a substitute for the woman's (the mother's) penis that the little boy once believed in and – for reasons familiar to us – does not want to give up.'[10] Rather than accept that women have no penises, and therefore that castration is a possibility, the boy/man fixates on some object which substitutes in his mind for the penis in whose existence he can no longer quite believe. In Mulvey's account, fixation on the female image in cinema is a kind of fetishism, indicating 'complete disavowal of castration by the substitution of a fetish object or turning the represented figure itself into a fetish so that it becomes reassuring rather than dangerous (hence over-valuation, the cult of the female star).'[11] The lingering glances of Bankes or Tansley at Mrs Ramsay – their freezing of her within picture- or window-frame – can be seen as a fetishistic denial of the danger that she really represents. Their fixation on her beauty, and their refusal to look further than the image, is proof that they are using her appearance – her 'represented figure' – as a screen for something more disturbing. But again this is her contradiction, and the contradiction of any fetish object. It seems to offer reassurance and protection; yet it is also a constant reminder of fear. Like the lighthouse, the fetish is on the interface between safety and danger.

It is not only in her exploration of the spectacle of femininity that Woolf's work anticipates contemporary film theory, however. Another concept critical to modern understanding of cinema, suture (literally, the stitching or joining of the lips of a wound), is also prefigured in her essay on cinema.

Suture is a term elaborated in Lacanian psychoanalysis. In film theory it comes to mean the constant reconstruction of the spectator/subject through each successive image of the film. The concept in classical cinema depends on the editing technique known as 'shot/reverse shot'. Stephen Heath explains this as follows.

> A reverse shot folds over the shot it joins and is joined in turn by the reverse it positions; a shot of a person looking is succeeded by a shot of the object looked at which is succeeded in turn by a shot of the person looking to confirm the object as seen; and so on, in a number of multiple imbrications.[12]

This is a way of moving the narrative forward in a coherent manner. Every shot is revealed to have an owner, a cause; there are no unclaimed perspectives (remember the ambiguous non-omniscient narrator who seems to be implied by some passages in *To the Lighthouse*).

Suture works by implying a point of view. As Annette Kuhn puts it: 'the source of cinematic enunciation is typically absent from, or invisible in, the text.'[13] In classic realist cinema, the projector is always behind us, and, in Kuhn's words, 'the narrator is not foregrounded as a "person"; "I" is not enunciated.'[14] This produces an absence which will be filled by the spectator, who becomes the subject of the look and whose point of view is actually represented in the film in the next image. It now appears that the spectators of the film are watching it from within the space of the film itself: as if they are actually there.

> What then operates, classically, is the effacement (or filling in)
> of the absence, the suturing of the discourse . . . by the reap-
> propriation of the absence within the film, a character in the
> film coming to take the place of the Absent One posed by the
> spectator.[15]

The shot/reverse shot structure means that we are drawn into
the film with the reverse shot which allows us to discover
from whose point of view the original shot was taken, and to
realise that we have ourselves been bound into the film's net-
work of looks by seeing from the position of the character
who now appears on screen.

All of Woolf's terms in 'The cinema' – pleasure, absence
and 'smoothing away' – are critical to the process of suture.
Heath reiterates Woolf's description of the initial pleasure of
the spectator.

> The process of reading a film goes in stages, the first of which is
> a moment of sheer jubilation *in* the image . . . a moment, as it
> were, untroubled by screen and frame, prior to the articulation
> of cinema. Awareness of the frame then breaks this initial rela-
> tion, the image now seen in its limits.[16]

The realisation that breaks this pleasure is one of absence. As
Woolf puts it, 'we behold [the images] as they are when we
are not there' (C, 269); in Heath's words, 'the spectator's
pleasure becomes a problem of representation, of being-
there-*for* – there for an absent field, outside of the image.'[17]
The spectator's absence is made good by a shot/reverse shot,
so that the spectator's point of view is taken up as a position
within the film. The spectator is 'knitted in' to its narrative
process. His or her absence from the film is, as Woolf said,
'smoothed away'.

Many of these processes are, as we have seen, reproduced
in *To the Lighthouse*. The suturing operation whereby
object becomes subject is a common device of the novel's
narrative, binding all the characters together into one
perspectival system. But the rhythm of suture – catching the
subject up as it is displaced – is reproduced in almost every
sentence.

Since he belonged, even at the age of six, to that great clan which cannot keep this feeling separate from that, but must let future prospects, with their joys and sorrows, cloud what is actually at hand . . . James Ramsay, sitting on the floor cutting out pictures from the illustrated catalogue of the Army and Navy Stores, endowed the picture of a refrigerator as his mother spoke with heavenly bliss. It was fringed with joy. (TL, 9)

The cadence falls away until it is suddenly caught up at the end. Woolf wrote in her notes for the novel: 'to precipitate feeling, there should be a sense of waiting, of expectation: the child waiting to go to the Lighthouse: the woman awaiting the return of the couple.'[18] This breathlessness and expectancy lasts for as long as Lily's picture is unfinished, but on a smaller scale it is apparent in almost every long sentence. Typically Woolf keeps the main verb until the end. 'Had there been an axe handy, a poker, or any weapon that would have gashed a hole in his father's breast and killed him, there and then, James would have seized it' (TL, 9). Again the pause is one of contingency – 'had there been' – the contingency with which Mrs Ramsay's opening words are associated. But Mrs Ramsay's comment (' "yes, of course" ') seems to expel contingency from James' world, and to remove the unsettling period of waiting – the experience of absence – that must necessarily pass before tomorrow comes. James always lets 'future prospects, with their joys and sorrows, cloud what is actually at hand' (TL, 9).

Charles Tansley is rescued by Mrs Ramsay from a feeling of being 'out of it', of waiting around: 'he was standing by the table, fidgeting with something, awkwardly, feeling himself out of things' (TL, 14). Mrs Ramsay is responsible not only for bringing people back into the activities – the narrative – of the day, but also for the fostering of potential, of hope: 'moving with an indescribable air of expectation, as if she were going to meet someone round the corner' (TL, 15). For a moment Tansley, singled out by Mrs Ramsay as the recipient of her confidences, is completed, released into a world of pleasure and achievement, 'a fellowship, a professorship, – he felt capable of anything and saw himself – but what was she looking at?' (TL, 16). She is looking at a kind of film, the pasting of a poster:

The vast flapping sheet flattened itself out, and each shove of the brush revealed fresh legs, hoops, horses, glistening reds and blues, until half the wall was covered with the advertisement of a circus; a hundred horsemen, twenty performing seals, lions, tigers. (TL, 16)

Mrs Ramsay and Tansley watch as the picture unfolds, and it turns out to be a representation of prodigious feats, on the limits of the possible – just what Tansley has felt Mrs Ramsay makes him capable of. The circus is a spectacle of danger. Mrs Ramsay, who rescues people from the limits of possibility, is instantly alert to it: 'it was terribly dangerous work for a one-armed man, she exclaimed, to stand on top of a ladder like that – his left arm had been cut off in a reaping machine two years ago' (TL, 16).

For Tansley, Mrs Ramsay arrests attention in much the same way that we saw earlier the image of woman can in film (this is an instance not of the sadistic, but of the over-valuing, fetishistic response). Mrs Ramsay is even framed as if she were on screen: she 'stood quite motionless for a moment against a picture of Queen Victoria wearing the blue ribbon of the Garter; and all at once he realised that it was this: it was this: – she was the most beautiful person he had ever seen' (TL, 18). Queen Victoria is important in order to situate Mrs Ramsay historically, as a member of the parent generation; but also to suggest that Mrs Ramsay, like Victoria, is simultaneously domesticated – wife and mother – and hor-rifying – a woman who controls the lives of men. The super-lative, 'the most beautiful', comes in as a kind of answer. Mrs Ramsay bounds Tansley's notion of what beauty can be, as an unsurpassable limit. Her loveliness is beyond meaning: 'with stars in her eyes and veils in her hair, with cyclamen and wild violets – what nonsense was he thinking?' (TL, 18). He is spoken for as he looks at her, producing language which is not his own. For her beauty is incomprehensible and inexpressible beyond a simple statement of its existence: 'she was the most beautiful person he had ever seen.' Outside meaning, her magnetism is the constant crisis of the novel. 'A man digging in a drain stopped digging and looked at her; let his arm fall down and looked at her' (TL, 18). The association of Mrs Ramsay with the wilting, and earlier the amputation, of male limbs is as close as Woolf will get to writing castration. As Mrs Ramsay passes all movement is stilled, and the characteristic raised hand of masculine judgement is helpless in the face of her sexual incommensurability.

The superlatives with which the novel continually works (Mrs Ramsay is noted for her tendency to exaggerate) give some scenes a mythical intensity. Mr Ramsay, returning from his expedition into the wastes of heroic metaphor ('the intensity of his isolation and the waste of ages and the perishing of the stars' [TL, 38]), pays tribute to Mrs Ramsay: 'Finally putting his pipe in his pocket and bending his magnificent head before her – who will blame him if he does homage to the beauty of the world?' (TL, 38). Makiko Minow-Pinkney argues that Mrs Ramsay's physicality – the inescapable beauty of her body – is also responsible for the rhetoricity of her language ('she said, the other day, something about "waves mountains high" ' [TL, 13]).

> At one level, woman represents the *body*, that substratum of materiality without which her husband's abstract creations could not exist but which also threatens to 'dish' them . . . . Yet, at another level, she is also the *irrational*, her everyday intellectual caprices being only a short distance from psychosis and insanity. While her husband's speculations involve a self-discipline of mutual entailment (from P to Q to R, in Ramsay's terms), hers are unconstrained, excessive. Female biology is simultaneously the opposite of the male intellect and the ground for intellect's dangerous liberation into fancy or madness.[19]

The female body stands for limit: the unavoidability of sex (in Mulvey's words, 'ultimately, the meaning of woman is sexual difference, the absence of the penis as visually ascertainable'[20]). As we have seen, one possible male response is sadism, repeated attempts to uncover the truth of women's bodies, and then to punish them for it. It is with a strange energy that Mr Ramsay, stopping by the window in Section 6, is provoked to verbal assault by his wife's disregard of the limits of the possible: 'He stamped his foot on the stone step. "Damn you," he said . . . without replying, dazed and blinded, she bent her head as if to let the pelt of jagged hail, the drench of dirty water, bespatter her unrebuked. There was nothing to be said' (TL, 34). Mr Ramsay's aggression – his fear of his wife – is the other side of his need for her, and he constantly returns to her in search of reassurance – a repeated re-enactment of the half-truth of fetishism.

Mr Ramsay comes to his wife as she sits with her youngest child – sign of her corporeality, her immersion in the life of the body, sex and childbirth – to ask for her sympathy (Section 7). It is an intensely physical, Oedipal bond that he disrupts. James is 'standing between her knees, very stiff' (TL, 39). This stiffness is disrupted into a flow of metaphor between husband and wife that resembles Tansley's encomium earlier on ('what nonsense was he thinking?' [TL, 18]) and which, in its extravagance, 'disturbed the perfect simplicity and good sense of [James'] relations with his mother' (TL, 38). James, as he stands there, feels the immediacy of his mother's body dispersed.

> So boasting of her capacity to surround and protect, there was scarcely a shell of herself left for her to know herself by; all was so lavished and spent; and James, as he stood stiff between her knees, felt her rise in a rosy-flowered fruit tree laid with leaves and dancing boughs into which the beak of brass, the arid scimitar of his father, the egotistical man, plunged and smote, demanding sympathy. (TL, 39)

Water, light, and trees are the governing figures of the Ramsays' encounter. Mrs Ramsay produces at the same time 'a rain of energy, a column of spray' and a 'burning', an illumination (TL, 38). Annis Pratt has identified three strands of imagery in the passage. The first is of erection and ejaculation, a movement upwards (this she links to the phallic lighthouse); the second is the movement around, the encircling receptiveness of Mrs Ramsay; and the third is the twofold plunging and sucking activity of the male 'beak of brass' (TL, 39).[21] In Pratt's view, the aim of the passage is 'to develop three inter-related sets of sexual images to portray a psychosexual adaption forced upon [Mrs Ramsay] by the circumstances of her marriage and times.'[22] The force of 'adaption' conceived of by Pratt originates in her sense that Mrs Ramsay is provided with the wrong sets of images: her 'creative organ' is phallic; she seems to ejaculate; her husband sucks as well as penetrates.[23] But this apparent confusion of images can be seen as an extravaganza which liberates the novel from the inflexibility of sexual difference, the apparent immobility – the outer limit – of anatomy. If images for the biology of sex can be exchanged between partners, as a kind of metaphorical play, the sexual is emancipated from the rigours of the anatomical into a fantastic linguistic adventure which has neither horizon nor limit.

At the end the Ramsays' edifice falls like a house of cards: 'Mrs Ramsay seemed to fold herself together, one petal closed in another, and the whole fabric fell in exhaustion upon itself' (TL, 40). The return to the body is 'disagreeable' precisely because Mrs Ramsay's function is to sustain a *falsely* unified identity for the men in the novel. 'She did not like, even for a second, to feel finer than her husband; and further, could not bear not being entirely sure, when she spoke to him, of the truth of what she said' (TL, 40). The sexual relation (and the relation of suture) is based on a kind of dishonesty, the untruth of vision and of fetishism: denying the crisis of subjectivity that is sexual difference. This is the difficulty of perspective that we have noted before – the dilemma of presence/absence: 'So that was the Lighthouse, was it? No, the other was also the Lighthouse. For nothing was simply one thing' (TL, 172). A fetish also, in Freud's words, is 'doubly derived from contrary ideas.'[24] As fetishism arises from a refusal to acknowledge what has been seen, so, in *To the Lighthouse*, the act of seeing always seems imbued with the hesitant 'divided attitude' of the fetishist.[25] Things are at once what they seem, and far from it. Even the opening exchange (Mrs Ramsay's ' "yes" ', Mr Ramsay's ' "but" ' [TL, 9]) echoes the classic recognition/denial of the fetishist: 'yes, in his mind the woman *has* got a penis, in spite of everything; but this penis is no longer the same as it was before.'[26]

There is a difficulty, however, with taking the fetishistic scene as prototypical of any kind of looking in the novel. Freud is quite clear that only men have fetishes. What happens when Lily gazes so intensely at Mrs Ramsay? This is a question that will be discussed more fully in Chapter 6; for the moment I shall indicate some of the answers. The colours that Lily sees are violent and intense: 'the jacmanna was bright violet; the wall staring white' (TL, 22). Even the act of looking is painful: 'with all her senses quickened as they were, looking, straining, till the colour of the wall and the jacmanna beyond burnt into her eyes' (TL, 21). This pain is the shock of attention, and the intensity of Lily's stare eclipses the gentle 'gazing' of the artist seen by Tansley and Mrs Ramsay. Where Lily is taking a risk, the artist is sitting 'seriously, softly, absorbedly . . . with an air of profound contentment on his round red face' (TL, 17), and where for Lily, to be looked at is agony, the artist seems hardly to notice 'that he was watched by ten little boys' (TL, 17). For Lily alone, Mrs Ramsay cannot perform the fetishistic function of reassurance.

Lily sees Mrs Ramsay not as a body but as a problem in perspective and relationship. Bankes, tapping her canvas in an echo of Mr Ramsay's striking with his 'beak of brass', asks Lily what the purple shape represents.

> It was Mrs Ramsay reading to James, she said. She knew his objection – that no one could tell it for a human shape. But she had made no attempt at likeness, she said. For what reason had she introduced them then? he asked. Why indeed? – except that if there, in that corner, it was bright, here, in this, she felt the

need of darkness . . . . The question being one of the relation of masses, of lights and shadows. (TL, 52)

The problem is again that of the kaleidoscope: how can Lily make her painting fall into place, locate Mrs Ramsay so that she makes sense? Mrs Ramsay gives Bankes the same pleasure as she gave to the other men, that of 'the solution of a scientific problem, so that he rested in contemplation of it, and felt, as he felt when he had proved something absolute about the digestive system of plants, that barbarity was tamed, the reign of chaos subdued' (TL, 47–8).

For Lily, however, watching Mrs Ramsay is not a comfort but a challenge. This is the difficulty of the female spectator of a feminine scene devised for men (Mrs Ramsay 'had the whole of the other sex under her protection' [TL, 11]). Mary Ann Doane, noting that spectatorial (fetishistic) pleasure demands distance – the distance insisted on by sexual difference, men looking at women – elucidates Lily's dilemma:

> For the female spectator there is a certain over-presence of the image – she *is* the image. Given the closeness of this relationship, the female spectator's desire can be described only in terms of a kind of narcissism – the female look demands a becoming.[27]

In other words, the female spectator is already sutured into the cinematic scene because she sees femininity – herself – fetishised there. In admiring femininity on screen, or that so triumphantly staged by Mrs Ramsay, the female spectator/Lily is checked by her own falling short of that unsurpassable limit. The confrontation between Lily and Mrs Ramsay in Section 9 underlines Lily's inadequacy: 'there could be no disputing this: an unmarried woman (she lightly took her hand for a moment), an unmarried woman has missed the best of life' (TL, 49). The secret language of the cinematic aesthetic which Woolf posed as a problem in her essay on cinema is also a question of the feminine relation to fetishism within the terms set up by the novel. How can Mrs Ramsay be a fetish for Lily? How can she reassure her when the narcissistic identification into which she invites her would involve an acceptance of a version of marriage and maternity that Lily already finds oppressive? Yet as the novel is constructed, with Mrs Ramsay as the prototype for the desired object of the gaze, there is no other narrative into which it is possible for the women in the novel to be bound. For the men – even the unmarried ones – this is exactly the closure they seek: knowing themselves confirmed in masculinity by the woman's narrative as wife and mother. Lily, however, is left in an impossible relation to looking. Her difficulties come to a head in the dinner party which follows.

4

The Dinner Party

The dinner party in Part I stands in for the rites of marriage. Mrs Ramsay presides over the distribution of food as she does over the arrangement of couples ('foolishly, she had set them opposite each other. That could be remedied tomorrow' [TL, 97]). The party is her 'triumph' – the word is repeated several times. Her children – proof of her right to claim precedence as wife and mother – deck her out.

It is Mrs Ramsay who initiates and sustains the narrative development, both within the scene itself and, on a larger scale, in her urging people on to marry. Movement is the responsibility of women. It is men who have watches (Mr Ramsay looks at the time [TL, 65]; Paul had 'found a gold watch' [TL, 73] as a child, and now has one 'in a wash-leather bag' [TL, 108]), but it is women who keep them ticking: 'giving herself the little shake that one gives a watch that has stopped' (TL, 79). Lily, earlier, saw her paints 'like clods with no life in them now, yet she vowed, she would inspire them, force them to move, flow, do her bidding tomorrow' (TL, 49). Mrs Ramsay, in her parallel creation of the dinner party, feels that 'the whole of the effort of merging and flowing and creating rested on her' (TL, 79). It is up to women to initiate circulation – of looks, talk, food.

The novel's narrative, as we saw in Chapter 3, is the working-out of a conflict in the position of women as both subjects and objects of the look. Mrs Ramsay is the novel's desired object (its aim is to represent and make sense of her both present and absent), but exactly by being its object she is also its subject, setting it in motion and dictating the shape it will take. Annette Kuhn calls such a function a 'woman-structure' in narrative:

> no longer is 'woman' regarded as a concrete gendered human being who happens to exist on the cinema screen rather than in 'real' life: 'she' becomes, on the contrary, a structure governing the organisation of story and plot in a narrative or group of narratives.[1]

This is just how Lily perceives Mrs Ramsay. She is exactly the problem of the structure of Lily's painting: where should she be placed, how related to the other objects in the scene?

Lily's other difficulty, as we saw at the end of the last chapter, is how to structure her own relation to Mrs Ramsay's 'woman-structure': the governing narrative of heterosexual marriage. Marriage is very frequently a plot closure in novel and film alike: 'narrative closure [in a sample of films from 1930s and 40s] is always dependent on the resolution of enigmas centring on heterosexual courtship.'[2] This is true also of Lily's painting. In finishing it she seems to offer definition of both Mrs Ramsay's and her own relation to heterosexuality. 'It is often woman – as structure, character, or both – who constitutes the motivator of the narrative, the "trouble" that sets the plot in motion.'[3] We have seen from Tansley's reactions on their shopping trip that Mrs Ramsay, with her power to arrest the gaze, can momentarily paper over the cracks in male self-esteem (although men continue to have private misgivings about the distractions of family life). But Lily, who with Mrs Ramsay bears the burden of the 'woman-structure', is deeply troubled by the dominance of marriage as a narrative. This chapter will explore marriage as a 'woman-structure' in the great set piece of the dinner party.

As Mrs Ramsay ceases reading, she sees in James' eyes, 'as the interest of the story died away in them, something else take its place; something wondering, pale, like the reflection of a light' (TL, 59). James' face reflects back the 'marvel' (TL,

60) of the rhythmic flash which announces the second half of the first part of the novel. The transition from sound to light – from Mrs Ramsay's voice to the beam of the lighthouse – echoes a change in the governing images of the book. Whereas in the first ten sections it is the sound of the waves that has emphasised Mrs Ramsay's sense of danger, in the last nine sections images of light inform the narrative, guiding it towards its triumphant end: 'And she looked at him smiling. For she had triumphed again' (TL, 114). Mrs Ramsay's victory is specular: 'And as she looked at him, she began to smile, for though she had not said a word, he knew, of course he knew, that she loved him' (TL, 114). Women are associated with illumination and spectacle. At Mrs Ramsay's request, instead of giggling at dinner, the children light candles – a kind of visual laughter (TL, 89). Light, like 'woman', keeps the narrative going against the threat of extinction.

The engagement of Paul and Minta, who arrive late from their walk on the beach, encourages others – Mrs Ramsay and Lily – to speculate on love and heterosexual union. Charles Tansley and Bankes seethe disgustedly at the chaos of family life, the way in which women disrupt the solitude and silence of the working routine. 'Mrs Ramsay had to break off here to tell the maid something about keeping food hot. All these interruptions annoyed him' (TL, 83), thinks William Bankes. The men at the beginning of the meal are deprived of uninterrupted contemplation of Mrs Ramsay's beauty, unable to repress the castration fear she arouses in them, through the over-valuing gaze of the fetishist. They compensate with aggression.

The neurotic fear of loss and of waste (linked to castration anxiety) – waste of energy, waste of food, waste of time – is central to this part of the book, and is associated with the fear of flooding water, encroaching darkness (images recalling the female genitals). The room with its long dining table, the empty plates 'making white circles' (TL, 78), is like a boat, and one of the images for waste is of the sinking ship, gradually obliterated by water and night. The candle-light reflected in the windows (no longer framing distant vistas) holds off the danger outside.

> Now all the candles were lit, and the faces on both sides of the table were brought nearer by the candle light, and composed, as they had not been in the twilight, into a party round a table, for the night was now shut off by panes of glass, which, far from giving any accurate view of the outside world, rippled it so strangely that here, inside the room, seemed to be order and dry land; there, outside, a reflection in which things wavered and vanished, waterily. (TL, 90–1)

The effect of the light is to distribute fluidity, to re-order substance. Again Mrs Ramsay is associated both with danger – the wet darkness of the female sexual parts – and also with the protective function: she orders candles to be lit, and presides over the table.

The distribution of fluidity through the arrangement of light can also be imaged as a climax at which 'woman' realises herself as perfectly female. Mrs Ramsay, left alone for a moment after James has been taken to bed, has a vision of perfection, of satiety. It is a fluid crescendo of colour:

> She thought, watching [the light] with fascination, hypnotized, as if it were stroking with its silver fingers some sealed vessel in her brain whose bursting would flood her with delight, she had known happiness, exquisite happiness, intense happiness, and it silvered the rough waves a little more brightly, as daylight faded, and the blue went out of the sea and it rolled in waves of pure lemon which curved and swelled and broke upon the beach and the ecstasy burst in her eyes and waves of pure delight raced over the floor of her mind and she felt, It is enough! It is enough! (TL, 62–3)

The lighthouse beam is an image for a pleasure that is partly sexual ('she woke in the night and saw it bent across their bed, stroking the floor' [TL, 62]) but which is also an acute delight in seeing, a chromatic ecstasy (remember the intensity of Lily's gaze). Mrs Ramsay's sexual organs are her eyes. Maria Dibattista has noted that women in this novel have a strong faith in transfiguration: painting, cooking, gardening.[4] Certainly Mrs Ramsay's vision is of a gradual transformation, in which the silver of sex drives out the blue of femininity and brings in its place the yellow that is associated with meditation and intoxication (Mr Carmichael 'took opium. The children said he had stained his beard yellow with it' [TL, 41]).[5] Blue and green hold Mrs Ramsay in her place as wife and mother: it is 'mounds of blue and green' (TL, 49) that Lily scrapes at earlier in her attempts to paint Mrs Ramsay; Mrs Ramsay 'folded the green shawl about her shoulders' (TL, 63) to walk with her husband. This blue and green are displaced by the 'lemon' of irresponsibility and hallucination. Mrs Ramsay's expectancy is resolved in a 'burst' of feeling that what she sees and what she is are perfectly in harmony: 'it is enough!' This sense of 'enough' is the epiphany against which the tragedy of short lives and short stockings, and of excess time and excess food, are weighed. Not too little and not too much. Mrs Ramsay's vision is of an exactness: a perfectly realised pleasure.

Mrs Ramsay's chromatic rapture is compared in the walk that follows it with the kinds of pleasure that her husband finds in the world around him. He passes her 'chuckling at the thought that Hume, the philosopher, grown enormously fat, had stuck in a bog' (TL, 62). His joy is in substance, masses. Gillian Beer says of this episode:

> The giant towering above [Mr Ramsay's] own endeavours as a philosopher proves to be a gross man subsiding. For a moment he can be held to scale, contained in anecdote. But . . . Hume's persistence, the fact that his difficulties cannot be disposed of, makes him a necessary part of the book's exploration of substance and absence, of writing as survival.[6]

In the novel's metaphysical register this is of course true. But Mr Ramsay's chuckle also raises the question of pleasure. Where Mrs Ramsay's 'ecstasy' (TL, 63) is in fluidity, transformation, colour, Mr Ramsay likes to think of the immovable ('the very stone one kicks with one's boot will outlast Shakespeare' [TL, 37]). Thinking of the limits to his knowledge, 'he braced himself. He clenched himself' (TL, 36). It is rigidity that will save Mr Ramsay, a resistance to movement, to being swept along from one position to another.

> Who then could blame the leader of that forlorn party which
> after all has climbed high enough to see the waste of the years
> and the perishing of stars, if before death stiffens his limbs
> beyond the power of movement he does a little consciously
> raise his numbed fingers to his brow, and square his shoulders,
> so that when the search party comes they will find him dead at
> his post, the fine figure of a soldier? Mr Ramsay squared his
> shoulders and stood very upright by the urn. (TL, 37)

The urn, of course, although it only holds geraniums, is a reminder of the disintegration of the body against which Mr Ramsay must brace himself. By forcing his body into an attitude of immobility and tension, he keeps at bay the imminent realisation of his own inadequacy. In the absence of Mrs Ramsay he must rely not on the look at another but on self-dramatisation. Mr Ramsay marks out the limits of human knowledge with a body that is as stiff as a board.

Watching himself is a game to Mr Ramsay. He clothes himself in words in an attempt to conceal his unease about his professional competence, weaving stories about being the leader of 'a desolate expedition across the icy solitudes of the Polar region' (TL, 36). His stories are realised physically; transformation for him, unlike for Mrs Ramsay, occurs not in what he sees but in what he is, as he stiffens by the urn. This ludic temperament gives him an extraordinary optimism, for there is no end to the meanings he can make.

> He said the most melancholy things, but she noticed that dir-
> ectly he had said them he always seemed more cheerful than
> usual. All this phrase-making was a game, [Mrs Ramsay]
> thought, for if she had said half what he said, she would have
> blown her brains out by now. (TL, 66)

This 'phrase-making' obscures Mr Ramsay's vision: his vision of loss, his vision of suffering, and even his fear and vision of castration. All Mr Ramsay's fantasies, annoying as they are to his wife, seem to help him resist decay (he is still potent – enviably so: 'his arm was almost like a young man's arm, Mrs

Ramsay thought, thin and hard, and she thought with delight how strong he still was, though he was over sixty' [TL, 67]), such that the Ramsays' walk can be, after all those years, a stroll through images of sexual delight, the 'two clumps of red-hot pokers' (TL, 65), the 'silver-green spear-like plants' (TL, 67).

As Lily watches them, they suddenly become 'the symbols of marriage, husband and wife' (TL, 69). This 'symbolical outline' (TL, 69) descends on them in the context of a cluster of images of capture which emphasise the narrative's – and marriage's – function to *contain* the subject, to dictate its position. Prue throws a ball high in the air; it escapes out of sight. 'There was a sense of things having been blown apart, of space, of irresponsibility as the ball soared high, and they followed it and lost it and saw the one star and the draped branches' (TL, 69). In Part II, things will be radically 'blown apart' by death and war, as the rook family in Part I is continually dispersed by Jasper's shooting. But here, as Prue catches her ball, things are brought back, netted, and the bodilessness – the freedom from the tyranny of flesh and sex that they have all momentarily experienced – is filled in again.

> Then, darting backwards over the vast space (for it seemed as if solidity had vanished altogether), Prue ran full tilt into them and caught the ball brilliantly high up in her left hand, and her mother said, 'Haven't they come back yet?' whereupon the spell was broken. (TL, 70)

Simultaneously, things are gathered back in – balls and people – and bodies regain their substance. The old rhythm of movement and collision begins again, and with it return the insistent demands of gender and marriage. People are no longer granted the irresponsibility of allowing things out of their sight, of escaping from a world of spectacle in which the castrated woman is only the most problematic of possible visual scenes. 'Mrs Ramsay, bringing Prue back into the alliance of family life again, from which she had escaped, throwing catches, asked, "Did Nancy go with them?" ' (TL,

70). This question is an effort at visualisation, a bringing of people back into her line of vision: 'she tried to recall the sight of them standing at the hall door after lunch' (TL, 54). It is the beginning of the process of collecting together, of returning people to their bodies, to their sex, into couples, into the family, that will climax when Mrs Ramsay presides over everyone at the dinner table, even Mr Bankes. ' "I have triumphed to-night" ' (TL, 69), she tells Lily.

Images of loss are also woven into the story of Paul and Minta's engagement. As Rose chooses her mother's jewels, Mrs Ramsay divines 'some buried, some quite speechless feeling that one had for one's mother at Rose's age' (TL, 77). This association echoes the fate of Minta's grandmother's brooch, lost on the shore and now covered by the incoming tide. The erasure of signs of a matriarchal heritage – symbolised in the case of both Rose and Minta by jewels – signals Minta's entry into the heterosexual world in which lights, associated with Mrs Ramsay and heterosexual femininity, come out one by one to mark the sinking of the pre-Oedipal ship. Minta weeps.

> It was her grandmother's brooch; she would rather have lost anything but that, and yet Nancy felt, though it might be true that she minded losing her brooch, she wasn't crying only for that. She was crying for something else. We might all sit down and cry, she felt. But she did not know what for. (TL, 73)

Minta's destiny – to mourn a loss she cannot even name – is prefigured in the brooch itself: 'a weeping willow, it was (they must remember it) set in pearls' (TL, 73). Her aimless weeping is a recognition that women do have something to lose when they acquiesce in their function in the 'woman-structure' of marriage. The imagery of burial echoes Freud's own imagery for the pre-Oedipal relationship of mother and daughter: 'our insight into this early, pre-Oedipus phase in girls comes to us as a surprise, like the discovery, in another field, of the Minoan–Mycenaean civilisation behind that of Greece.'[7]

A Reading of the Text

It is Lily who manages to preserve a memory of this buried civilisation in her sense that there are hidden 'in the chambers of the mind and heart of the woman who was, physically, touching her . . . tablets bearing sacred inscriptions' (TL, 50). But even Lily, staunch as she is in her rejection of marriage, no longer has easy access to the pre-Oedipal. In struggling with her heterosexual destiny she has been somehow deprived, so that perfect intimacy with Mrs Ramsay constantly eludes her: 'nothing happened. Nothing! Nothing! as she leant her head against Mrs Ramsay's knee' (TL, 51).

At the beginning of the meal the prevailing atmosphere is one of antagonism between the sexes, a feeling of failed communication. In this dinner, that is consecrated to the celebration of heterosexuality, such tensions are inevitable. Lily's despair at the falsity with which she comes to Tansley's rescue ('she would never know him. He would never know her. Human relations were all like that, she thought' [TL, 86]) is a criticism of Mrs Ramsay as well as an echo of Mrs Ramsay's discontent earlier at the dishonesty of her conjugal relation. Bankes, failed by Mrs Ramsay, feels the whole thing a terrible 'waste of time' (TL, 83): even Mrs Ramsay's 'beauty meant nothing to him' (TL, 83). Tansley thinks that he is being 'made a fool of by women' (TL, 81); 'They did nothing but talk, talk, talk, eat, eat, eat. It was the women's fault' (TL, 81). Tansley characteristically obstructs Lily's view: 'he sat opposite to her with his back to the window precisely in the middle of view' (TL, 80). Bankes begins to ask questions about sex. 'Why, one asked oneself, does one take all these pains for the human race to go on?' (TL, 84). Faced with Mrs Ramsay's exaltation at the thought of Paul and Minta's approaching marriage, all three guests, initially, rebel against embracing the same destiny for themselves.

For all three, work is presented as a refuge from sex. Much earlier, Lily has already felt something of the kind, taking up 'once more her old painting position with the dim eyes and the absent-minded manner, subduing all her impressions as a woman to something much more general' (TL, 52). All three protect themselves from imputations of sexual inadequacy with thoughts of their work. 'He has his work, Lily said to herself. She remembered, all of a sudden as if she had found a treasure, that she too had her work' (TL, 80). Work is instead of family, instead of sex; indeed, Tansley's feeling that work and family are mutually exclusive ('of course Ramsay had dished himself by marrying a beautiful woman and having eight children' [TL, 85]) is echoed throughout the novel by other characters as well. Work, which is a kind of private and uninterrupted perspective, is cherished like a child. Lily wants to 'clasp some miserable remnant of her vision to her breast' (TL, 23), in an echo of Mrs Ramsay, who also hates to be thwarted, and feels safe only with a baby in her arms (TL, 57). Lily's intervention in the arrangements for the meal is to '[take] up the salt-cellar and put it down again on a flower in the pattern in the table-cloth, so as to remind herself to move the tree' (TL, 80). The salt-cellar is substituted for Mrs Ramsay – now unsatisfactory, in her frightening and confusing demands ('she put a spell on them all, by wishing, so simply, so directly' [TL, 94]) – as Lily's focal point, towards which all her dreams and designs tend.

But Lily's displacement of Mrs Ramsay and marriage by the salt-cellar in her own counter-narrative does not last for long. The lighting of the candles heralds the entrance of the lovers (Mrs Ramsay's 'uneasiness changed to expectation' [TL, 91]). The beautiful 'yellow and purple dish of fruit' (TL, 90) revealed in the candle-light is an expression of the colour, fertility and sense of possibility which Paul and Minta bring into the room with them. Jack Stewart notes that purple, the combination of red and blue, masculine and feminine, is the 'chromatic signifier of integration' in the novel.[8] Yellow, as we have seen, is the colour of intoxication, the colour of opium stains. The fruit is linked to Bacchanalian rites.

> What had she done with it, Mrs Ramsay wondered, for Rose's arrangement of the grapes and pears, of the horny pink-lined shell, of the bananas, made her think of a trophy fetched from the bottom of the sea, of Neptune's banquet, of the bunch that

hangs with vine leaves over the shoulder of Bacchus (in some picture), among the leopard skins and the torches lolloping red and gold. . . . Thus brought up suddenly into the light it seemed possessed of great size and depth, was like a world in which one could take up one's staff and climb up hills, she thought, and go down into valleys. (TL, 90)

The candle-light, the illumination of the bowl of fruit, and the couplings that are arranged at this meal co-operate to hold off the dark formlessness and the floods that threaten outside the windows. In looking at the fruit the recalcitrant guests are bound back into admiration of the spectacle of marriage: 'Augustus too feasted his eyes on the same plate of fruit . . . looking together united them' (TL, 90). The fruit represents festival and irresponsibility, Bacchanalian orgies, the bringing together of the pears of masculine thought (Bankes earlier paused 'by the pear tree, well brushed, scrupulously exact, exquisitely judicial' [TL, 27]) and the 'torch' (TL, 42) of feminine beauty. It functions like Lily's picture ('in some picture') in focusing attention and establishing the hegemony of heterosexual relationship: the vaginal 'pink-lined shell'; the phallic bananas. What is more it encourages hope, invites exploration, seeming to offer – as does marriage – a new, exciting, yet safe, panorama.

But there is, of course, a danger. The 'pink-lined shell' is horny, holding the threat of castration; Bacchanalian orgies are violent and destructive as well as ecstatic. The figure with the staff travelling the hills is reminiscent of Hercules, who was not well served by women or by marriage. Later the Ramsays and their guests will talk of *Anna Karenina* (TL, 100) and, by implication, the cruelty of sexual relationships. Minta never got to the end of *Middlemarch* (TL, 91), leaving Dorothea stranded in the wastes of life with Casaubon. Mrs Ramsay almost gloats, serving out the meat:

[She] thought, This will celebrate the occasion – a curious sense rising in her, at once freakish and tender, of celebrating a festival, as if two emotions were called up in her, one profound – for what could be more serious than the love of man for woman, what more commanding, more impressive, bearing in its bosom the seeds of death; at the same time these lovers, these people entering into illusion glittering eyed, must be danced round with mockery, decorated with garlands. (TL, 93)

Mrs Ramsay knows that marriage is deathly as well as life-giving. The picture that Paul and Minta see together is fraught with falsity – the falsity of the sexual relation, the dishonesty of vision – and their love carries with it – as does Mrs Ramsay's beauty – the threat of mortality and of loss.

Lily guesses something of Mrs Ramsay's knowledge: 'there was something frightening about her. She was irresistible' (TL, 94). To Lily the 'red and gold' (TL, 90) of the fruit, Minta's 'golden-reddish' haze (TL, 92), are the destructive 'heat of love, its horror, its cruelty, its unscrupulosity. It scorched her' (TL, 95). But it is partly this danger that Lily craves: 'how inconspicuous she felt herself by Paul's side! He, glowing, burning; she, aloof, satirical; he, bound for adventure; she, moored to the shore; he, launched, incautious; she solitary, left out' (TL, 94). Instead of going in a boat, Lily will, in Part III, paint her picture. The exhilaration of work will substitute for the danger and excitement of sex. But Lily is not entirely content. On the one hand she is dissatisfied with what she knows of love: 'women, judging from her own experience, would all the time be feeling, This is not what we want' (TL, 95). Work seems like a peaceful and exciting retreat. Yet she envies Paul and Minta, feeling that love is 'beautiful and necessary' (TL, 95). Lily cannot resolve her dilemma, 'to feel violently two opposite things at the same time' (TL, 95). In a sense this is the tendency of the book, to provoke such a feeling, such an unsettledness. We remember that Woolf wanted the novel to close on 'the sense of reading the two things at the same time' (D, III, 5 September 1926, 106).

It is the function of Mrs Ramsay to smooth over that division. A skull – like the 'seeds of death' – is nailed on the wall of the children's bedroom. 'Cam couldn't get to sleep with it in the room, and James screamed if she touched it' (TL, 105). By winding her shawl around the skull, Mrs Ramsay manages to make it simultaneously skull and not-skull. Cam no longer has to see the 'horrid thing, branching at her all over the room' (TL, 106) (shadows turn it into a phallic nightmare), but James knows that 'the boar's skull was still there' (TL, 106). This veiling is again characteristic of fetishism, not only because the fetishist attempts to hide his knowledge from himself, but also because clothing is so often adopted as the fetish object (and plays a vital part in the construction of femininity as spectacle): 'pieces of underclothing, which are so often chosen as a fetish, crystallise the moment of undressing, the last moment in which the woman could still be regarded as phallic.'[9] Mrs Ramsay clothes the skull, reminder of death and sex, in a way that produces the classic fetish object, one which allows simultaneous recognition and denial of fear. That it is her own shawl that she winds around the boar's head only serves to strengthen her own association with the fetish. Now Cam and James can each choose what to believe about the skull: for one it is absent, for the other, present.

Lily's difficulty – that of being at once in and not in the 'woman-structure' of the narrative which tends to bind her in marriage – forces her constantly to negotiate the dilemma of absent presence. At the dinner party the negotiation comes to a head in the domestic setting, maintained as a shrine to marriage and heterosexual femininity. The second part of the novel takes up the crisis of absent presence when the fetishising function fails – when Mrs Ramsay is dead and the house begins to break up. This is the most ambitious section of the novel, and the most experimental. In the next chapter we shall look more closely at its techniques.

5

Time Passing

The strange middle section of *To the Lighthouse*, 'Time Passes', was a part of Woolf's plans for the book even before she had started writing it. It was one of the difficulties she most looked forward to working with: 'A new problem like that breaks fresh ground in ones mind; prevents the regular ruts' (D, III, 20 July 1925, 36). She also meant it to break up the novel, 'this impersonal thing, which I'm dared to do by my friends, the flight of time, & the consequent break of unity in my design' (D, III, 20 July 1925, 36). 'Time Passes' would crack the stable ground laid with such care in the first half. Continuity would be destroyed; the plot of the novel despoiled.

Whereas the first part is concerned with the construction of the human gaze, the relationship of watcher to the scene that is watched, in the second part there is no longer anyone watching. Narrative is realised simply through the passage of time.

Human events bear witness to historical change: marriage, childbirth, death. But without any spectators, the status of the human event is problematic. Woolf herself was puzzled by 'Time Passes' while she was writing it:

> I cannot make it out – here is the most difficult abstract piece of writing – I have to give an empty house, no people's characters, the passage of time, all eyeless & featureless with nothing to cling to: well, I rush at it, & at once scatter out two pages. Is it nonsense, is it brilliance? Why am I so flown with words, & apparently free to do exactly what I like? (D, III, 18 April 1926, 76)

The absence from the second part of the novel of people looking exposes it to the danger of structurelessness. This chapter will explore the ways in which Part II of *To the Lighthouse* manages to resist this threat.

In 'Time Passes' there is no focused gaze. The look here is either unseeing and nightmarish ('the trees standing there, and the flowers standing there, looking before them, looking up, yet beholding nothing, eyeless, and thus terrible' [TL, 125–6]), or it is distorted ('her eyes fell on nothing directly, but with a sidelong glance' [TL, 121]). As gazes slide away, there is no longer any stable system of perspective, no exchange of looks into which the spectator can be inserted: no possibility of suture. Projections are unstable and wandering.

> Faint and flickering, like a yellow beam or the circle at the end of a telescope, a lady in a grey cloak, stooping over her flowers, went wandering over the bedroom wall, up the dressing-table, across the washstand, as Mrs McNab hobbled and ambled, dusting, straightening. (TL, 127)

Mrs Ramsay, who used to flash on her beholders like a certainty, now flickers unstably in a world which denies the primacy of the human gaze. 'Time Passes' is the extreme of the cinematic scene with which Woolf was so fascinated: 'we see life as it is when we have no part in it' (C, 269).

Human answers – human meanings – are irrelevant in the world of Part II. Mrs Ramsay's narrative – marriage, child-birth and death – appears in brackets because it is displaced from the dark hellish atmosphere of the unpeopled island. The sleepers – not necessarily human – who pace the beach to ask questions of the waves – those waves which have had so many meanings for Mrs Ramsay – are forced in the end to admit that when they look out to sea their gaze is blankly reflected back, not taken up or woven in.

> That dream, then, of sharing, completing, finding in solitude on the beach an answer, was but a reflection in a mirror, and the mirror itself was but the surface glassiness which forms in quiescence when the nobler powers sleep beneath? (TL, 125)

The human subject has completely disappeared from this passage: it is both 'eyeless' and 'I-less'. Nature, a dream, and pacing the beach are the subjects of this section. They are illusions or actions (present participles) with no one to claim them.

Mirrors, so important in this passage, are to be avoided in the novel. 'Which did indeed? said Mrs Ramsay absent-mindedly, looking at her neck and shoulders (but avoiding her face), in the glass' (TL, 76). To look at her face will be to face the truth of the fading of her beauty, and the crisis in the subject that is dramatised in narcissism, the contemplation of the self. Mirrors carry no promise of future meanings, but rather a message of waste and mismanagement: 'when she looked in the glass and saw her hair grey, her cheek sunk, at fifty, she thought, possibly she might have managed things better – her husband; money; his books' (TL, 11–12). The mirror is saying that there are things it is beyond her power to manage: age, death, decay. It highlights the dishonesty with which her beauty as fetish persuades others that there is nothing to fear.

In the first part of the novel almost all looks engage with an object. In 'Time Passes' the looker is trapped in a self-enclosed universe without meaning and without relationship. The waves that meant so much to Mrs Ramsay have died down leaving a stagnant sea without life or movement, simply a 'surface glassiness', a hall of mirrors. Beauty – like Mrs Ramsay's – is exposed as a deceit, a false answer. The dream of a gaze that actually locates its object and achieves completion and response is shattered, just as the idyll of the family has been destroyed. 'Contemplation was unendurable; the mirror was broken' (TL, 125).

The storm and the floods of Part II are the dangers in whose shadow Part I took place. We have seen how the composed scene of the candle-lit dinner held off the encroaching fluidity outside. With the extinguishing of the lights in the house darkness floods in: the nightmare has begun. One of the aims of 'Time Passes' is to find a language for the unconscious, for sleep and dreams. Although we know that years have gone by (Lily is 33 in Part I, 44 in Part III), the span of Part II is also a single night. It opens with Lily and the others lying down to sleep; it closes with her 'sitting bolt upright in bed. Awake' (TL, 133). The cosmic convulsions of Part II, the years that seem to have passed, could be simply the fantasies, the accelerated time and exaggerated emotion of the dreamer. Woolf's project here is partly similar to that of James Joyce in his book of a day and of the conscious mind, *Ulysses* (1922), and his book of the night and of sleep, *Finnegans Wake* (1939). Woolf, approaching the problem on a smaller scale, compressed her two experiments into one book.

Although 'Time Passes' is a 'break of unity in [the] design' (D, III, 20 July 1925, 36), it is not entirely discontinuous from what comes before and after, any more than is the death of Mrs Ramsay. As we have seen, however, in Part II the characters no longer carry the chronology. Instead the narrative follows the rhythm of the sun and of the seasons, and the two governing images of Part I, the sea and the lighthouse, remain dominant. Part II opens with the withdrawal of the human gaze from the scene. The open eye of the lighthouse, warning ships from the rocks, is implicitly contrasted with the closed eyes of the sleepers. Sleep, the relaxation of vigilance, allows darkness and meaninglessness to seep in and fray the seams – the sutures – of the house and of human identity.

> Nothing, it seemed, could survive the flood, the profusion of darkness which, creeping in at keyholes and crevices, stole round window blinds, came into bedrooms, swallowed up here a jug and basin, there a bowl of red and yellow dahlias, there the sharp edges and firm bulk of a chest of drawers. Not only was furniture confounded; there was scarcely anything left of body or mind by which one could say 'This is he' or 'This is she'. (TL, 117)

The darkness eats away at the sharp corners of the furniture as later damp will rot the books. This is what happens in a house deserted by humans. Watching, alone, is what saves the fabric of human life from decay; watching is what knits together the wandering threads of houses and lives.

In this section, as in the dinner party before, it becomes possible to speak of darkness and water as if they were the same substance. Both trickle through keyholes, both distort and erase contours. In a novel which works with a series of composed scenes – shapes brought into significant relationship – the challenge to form that the darkness and the water represent is peculiarly menacing. It is not only the subject of the look – the human eye – that has been marginalised by the coming of night. The object too – corners, angles, colours – has been thrown into disarray. Furniture and people are suddenly unrecognisable. Gesture and voice become involuntary spasms rather than part of a continuing narrative: 'sometimes a hand was raised as if to clutch something or ward off something, or somebody groaned, or somebody laughed aloud as if sharing a joke with nothingness' (TL, 117). The raised hand of masculine judgement, the agonised groans of Mr Ramsay's solitude, the laughter of Mrs Ramsay's maternal gaiety, are mocked and reduced to mere stirrings of the flesh. Body has eschewed meaning and become simply substance.

Section 3 concerns itself with the frame. It is as though a picture has been unveiled only to be hidden again (Woolf refers in her essay on cinema to film-makers as 'picture-makers' [C, 269]).

> It seemed now as if, touched by human penitence and all its toil, divine goodness had parted the curtain and displayed behind it, single, distinct, the hare erect; the wave falling; the boat rocking, which, did we deserve them, should be ours always. But alas, divine goodness, twitching the cord, draws the curtain; it does not please him; he covers his treasures in a drench of hail, and so breaks them, so confuses them that it seems impossible that their calm should ever return or that we should ever compose from their fragments a perfect whole or read in the littered pieces the clear words of truth. For our penitence deserves a glimpse only; our toil respite only. (TL, 119)

The closeness of this passage to the question of cinema in Woolf's mind is demonstrated in the echo of images from 'The cinema': 'the wave falling; the boat rocking' is close to 'watching the boat sail and the wave break, we have time to open our minds wide to beauty' (C, 269). Even the suggestion of erection ('the hare erect') is present in the essay: 'now and again some vast form heaves itself up and seems about to haul itself out of chaos' (C, 268). The most significant parallel comes near the end of 'The cinema': 'sometimes at the cinema in the midst of its immense dexterity and enormous technical proficiency, the curtain parts and we behold, far off, some unknown and unexpected beauty. But it is for a moment only' (C, 272). The problem of the momentary insight in *To the Lighthouse* is also the problem of the cinematic scene, tempting Woolf to speculate about the evolution of a new language: 'Here is a scene waiting a new art to be transfixed' (C, 272). She sees intimations of the new art not in technological efficiency, but in technological disturbance. At one performance she attended, a fault in the projector meant that a tadpole shape on the screen 'swelled to an immense size, quivered, bulged, and sank back again into nonentity' (C, 270). It seemed to be 'fear itself' (C, 270), to offer the possibility of an emotional language that would dispense with human narrative and the exigencies of character. In the absence of an adequate development of the filmic idiom, Woolf, in 'Time Passes', tried to do it herself.

The pictures that are revealed and then removed in Part II are ones that we recognise from Part I: 'The autumn trees gleam in the yellow moonlight, in the light of the harvest moons, the light which mellows the energy of labour, and smooths the stubble, and brings the wave lapping blue to the shore' (TL, 119). This is reminiscent of Mrs Ramsay's ecstatic vision of colour earlier. On her way downstairs from the children's room she has paused to look at 'the yellow harvest moon' (TL, 107). The impersonal world of Part II is still working with the same lexicon of images, but introducing them without the shaping influence of the spectator in the text. The excuse for that in the story, but also the significance of the change, is death. The transition from harvest moon to storm ('The nights now are full of wind and destruction; the trees plunge and bend' [TL, 119]) is at once an image for the wasting of all beauty (which finds an echo in the human world with the death of Mrs Ramsay at the end of the section), and for the changing of the seasons. But the inevitability with which the seasons change drives home the inescapability of death. Autumn fading into winter has a sinister as well as a benign effect. Substance, the flesh on which we have been so reliant, begins to waste. 'The hand dwindles in his hand; the voice bellows in his ear' (TL, 120).

This wasting of flesh prefigures the exodus of family and guests from the house: 'the house empty and the doors locked and the mattresses rolled round' (TL, 120). Now the absence of the human body is indicated by the empty shapes which it once inhabited:

> What people had shed and left – a pair of shoes, a shooting cap, some faded skirts and coats in wardrobes – those alone kept the human shape and in the emptiness indicated how once they were filled and animated. (TL, 120)

Again this is the absent presence of the cinematic image, where the human body is present not as substance but as two-dimensional shadow. The storms have died down. All that is left is the absolute stasis of the empty house. The convulsions of gales, winter, the dying of Mrs Ramsay, all have been succeeded by the silence of absence, of shapes without animation or spectators. 'So loveliness reigned and stillness, and together made the shape of loveliness itself, a form from which life had parted' (TL, 120–1). The images are all feminine (in the terms of this novel): mantles, folds, veils. There is no longer any colour, for colour means life. Instead the house is a cluster of moving light and darkness, the black and white of the early cinema: 'the shadows of the trees, flourishing in the wind, made obeisance on the wall, and for a moment darkened the pool in which light reflected itself' (TL, 120). The shadows projected on the wall are like images cast in an empty cinema. Light is not received but simply reflected back, bending 'to its own image

in adoration on the bedroom wall' (TL, 121). The w̄
glance of narcissism, that Mrs Ramsay was so careful to
avoid, permeates the house in the absence of the object. This
is a world without human subject, in which the dialectic of
subject and object has been lost altogether.

The illusions of the marriage narrative are gradually shattered as 'one fold of the shawl loosened and swung to and fro'
(TL, 121), the shawl that has concealed the death's head and
represented Mrs Ramsay's transfiguring maternal care. The
entry of Mrs McNab is the incursion of a counter-narrative
for women, but it is a very different one from that yearned for
by Lily. Makiko Minow-Pinkney comments that Mrs McNab
is:

> more Nature than Culture, a fact attested to by her difficulty in
> walking. . . . In contrast to her husband, Mrs Ramsay repres-
> ents Nature, but in contrast with McNab she is associated with
> an effete bourgeois culture against the more robust face of
> Nature itself.[1]

It is certainly true that where Mrs Ramsay's attempts to hold
off death – the winding shawl – fail and the shawl loosens,
Mrs McNab in her 'witlessness' (TL, 122) defeats decay
simply by being so much there – rather as Mr Ramsay would
have wished, 'tearing the veil of silence with hands that had
stood in the wash-tub, grinding it with boots that had
crunched the shingle' (TL, 121). In spite of her difficulties
with walking, Mrs McNab's feet are firmly on the ground.

Woolf's sense of her own class superiority is demonstrated
by the fact that in spite of the presence on the scene of Mrs
McNab, and later Mrs Bast, she can still feel that 'Time Passes'
is devoid of human character, and eyeless. The obliquity of
Mrs McNab's gaze is directly allied to her class and her ignorance: 'her eyes fell on nothing directly, but with a sidelong
glance that deprecated the scorn and anger of the world – she
was witless, she knew it' (TL, 121). Because her look cannot
organise, 'her sidelong leer which slipped and turned aside even
from her own face' (TL, 122), she is without power; or,

because she is subordinate, she cannot see. (Mrs McNab is an example of what Mary Ann Doane calls 'the negation of the female gaze' by the hegemony of class.[2]) The formlessness of Mrs McNab's world is echoed in the formlessness of her body, 'toothless, bonneted' (TL, 122). She is the raw material which the middle-class look shapes and informs: 'all of a sudden, would Mrs McNab see that the house was ready, one of the young ladies wrote: would she get this done; would she get that done; all in a hurry' (TL, 129). Resistance to orders comes not from Mrs McNab herself, but from the dead weight of her flesh. 'Mrs McNab groaned; Mrs Bast creaked. They were old; they were stiff; their legs ached . . . . Slowly and painfully, with broom and pail, mopping, scouring, Mrs McNab, Mrs Bast stayed the corruption and the rot' (TL, 129). Paradoxically, the women, whose bodies are themselves degenerate (another class projection) are nonetheless capable of checking the progress of decay elsewhere. They take on themselves the mortality of the rich, transferring symptoms of disintegration from the house to themselves. Where Mrs Ramsay has transformed objects by adroit concealment and imagination, Mrs McNab and Mrs Bast preside over a painful and entirely physical resurrection. The cleaning of the house is slow and difficult, the kind of labour in which Mrs Ramsay, with all her responsibilities, has never had to engage.

Kate Flint points out that the dates of composition of 'Time Passes' coincide almost exactly with the dates of the General Strike of 1926.[3] She suggests that the turmoil and uncontrollability of the darkened island are an expression of Woolf's profound anxiety at the disturbance to her world caused by the strike. The hierarchies and labour structures on which she had relied suffered severe disruption. Woolf, who for all her sympathies with the underdog had been accustomed to dominance as a member of the ruling class, now found the world she had been used to managing beginning to manage itself, and not necessarily in her interest. The turbulence of the sea perhaps indicates Woolf's anxiety at the restlessness of the working classes who have hitherto seemed so malleable. The nightmare of the stormy night is Woolf's premonition of social, as well as climatic, anarchy. As Flint says, the destruction of this one house symbolises a far deeper destruction, of the values that houses like the Ramsays' represent.[4]

The amenability of Mrs McNab and Mrs Bast is almost a wish fulfilment. Woolf's belief in their changelessness ('the voice of witlessness, humour, persistency itself, trodden down but springing up again' [TL, 122]) flies in the face of her experience of the desire of many workers to transform labour relations by making themselves deliberately unreliable. Mrs McNab seems to accept with only a ritual complaint the repetitiveness of her life and particularly of her work: 'as she lurched, dusting, wiping, she seemed to say how it was one long sorrow and trouble, how it was getting up and going to bed again, and bringing things out and putting them away again' (TL, 122). Compare this view of a working-class relation to routine with the way in which the everyday occasion of dinner at the Ramsays' is turned into a unique festival in celebration of middle-class life (the *Boeuf en Daube*, the candles). Although it is the cook who has worked on the *Boeuf en Daube*, the dish is, in the end, Mrs Ramsay's triumph.

The complicated relation that existed between members of Woolf's class and their servants is evident in these passages. Cooks and maids clothed, fed and washed them. They thus took on the reassuring status of the mother while being simultaneously degraded by their subordinate status. Yet, as Minow-Pinkney emphasises, there is, alongside the emotional tangles of the mistress and her maid, a liberating tendency here. Mrs McNab 'is envied for her liberation from a stultifying feminine role – hence the crazy energy that attaches to her despite her physical deformities.'[5] One can of course object that doing housework can at times be an enormously stultifying feminine role. But Mrs McNab is at least released by her very grotesqueness (by her class) from carrying the burden of femininity. She comes off duty when her work is finished and then spends her time drinking and gossiping

(TL, 122). Mrs Ramsay, by contrast, must continually work on herself. Her beauty and her femininity are her labour, and are therefore inescapable.

The marriage and death of Prue which follow the first entrance of Mrs McNab seem in some way to be a comment on this. Mrs Ramsay is always urging on the narrative of heterosexual femininity. The fate of Prue brings its dangers into stark relief. Mrs McNab's opacity and persistence are in implicit contrast with the delivering up of the limpid Prue to sex:

> the spring without a leaf to toss, bare and bright like a virgin fierce in her chastity, scornful in her purity, was laid out on the fields wide-eyed and watchful and entirely careless of what was done or thought by the beholders. (TL, 122–3)

Prue's marriage is a ritual sacrifice. Mrs Ramsay 'somehow laughed, led her victims, Lily felt, to the altar' (TL, 94). So Prue/the spring loses her defiance, 'softened and acquiescent' (TL, 123), and passes into summer with a gesture that recalls Mrs Ramsay, whose role as sexually mature woman Prue now doubles: 'threw her cloak about her, veiled her eyes, averted her head' (TL, 123). Mrs Ramsay of course knows death, and Prue will be initiated simultaneously into heterosexuality, maternity and dying: 'Prue Ramsay died that summer in some illness connected with childbirth' (TL, 123).

The General Strike is not the only national crisis represented in 'Time Passes'. The disturbances of the Great War shake the foundations of even this distant house, which will loose one of its sons, Andrew. The senselessness of the war stains the mirror-like surface of the sea – representing the cruel narcissism of nationalism. 'There was a purplish stain upon the bland surface of the sea as if something had boiled and bled, invisibly, beneath' (TL, 124). The purple of love and integration has been horribly tainted – 'purplish' – by the dealing of death to sons of families like the Ramsays. The collective insanity of the war disrupts even the natural rhythms of the waves, which become:

> like the amorphous bulks of leviathans whose brows are
> pierced by no light of reason, and mounted one on top of
> another, and lunged and plunged in the darkness or the
> daylight (for night and day, month and year ran shapelessly
> together) in idiot games, until it seemed as if the universe were
> battling and tumbling, in brute confusion and wanton lust
> aimlessly by itself. (TL, 125)

The rhythms of love, which have previously ordered the Ramsays' universe, are now as empty and mad as the irregular thud of the guns.

The 'wanton lust' of the waves is reflected in the fate of Ramsays' home. Even Mrs McNab finally deserts it: 'it was too much for one woman, too much, too much' (TL, 127). A crazy dispensation to breed governs the house. It is Mrs Ramsay's mania for marriage gone out of control, exaggerated as she herself was prone to become at times: 'let the wind blow; let the poppy seed itself and the carnation mate with the cabbage' (TL, 128). One form of life has decayed ('there were things up there rotting in the drawers' [TL, 128]) and another begins to take over: 'what power could now prevent the fertility, the insensibility of nature?' (TL, 128). The disintegrating props of human order spill out on the lawn: 'let the broken glass and the china lie out on the lawn and be tangled over with grass and wild berries' (TL, 129). It is only just in time that Mrs McNab and Mrs Bast arrive to begin the process of recuperation. Otherwise the tide that started out as rain and darkness, and is now the gradual encroaching of plants and grasses, would have entirely obliterated the house. 'Briars and hemlocks would have blotted out path, step, and window; would have grown, unequally but lustily over the mound' (TL, 129). But with the labour of Mrs McNab and Mrs Bast order is restored, and, simultaneously, the sea dies down and the national conflict is over. 'Then indeed peace had come. Messages of peace breathed from the sea to the shore' (TL, 132). The 'long night' (TL, 128) is finished. Human eyes are restored to their proper primacy, and Lily Briscoe finally awakens: 'her eyes opened wide' (TL, 133). Someone is keeping guard again.

6

Getting to the Lighthouse

In Part III, a party including the Ramsays (those who are left), Lily, and Mr Carmichael return to the house. Mr Ramsay takes James and Cam on the long-postponed trip to the lighthouse; Lily finishes her previously abandoned painting. The action is much tighter, the points of view fewer than in the first part of the novel. The absence of the dead Mrs Ramsay has caused a kind of tunnel vision. Looks occur only along one plane: between the Ramsays' home and the lighthouse.

Those allowed access to the gaze are also fewer. Mitchell Leaska, in his percentage analysis of the distribution of points of view in the novel, found that 50 per cent of Part I was seen through the eyes of Mrs Ramsay, and 60 per cent of Part III through the eyes of Lily.[1] It is as if one has been substituted for the other – and indeed, this is how Lily feels. As Mr Ramsay bears down on her, she senses that with Mrs Ramsay gone it is she who must bear the burden of womanhood: 'Surely she could imitate from recollection the glow, the rhapsody, the self-surrender she had seen on so many women's faces (on Mrs Ramsay's, for instance) when on some occasion like this they blazed up' (TL, 141). Lily is preoccupied throughout Part III with establishing her precise relation to Mrs Ramsay and her version of femininity, a relation that will define her position as narcissistic female spectator and, finally, lead her to reject contemplation of Mrs Ramsay altogether.

The problem for Lily as spectator/artist is that in admiring Mrs Ramsay, she is also sucked into conforming with her. We remember Mary Ann Doane's words, already cited in Chapter 3:

> for the female spectator there is a certain over-presence of the image – she *is* the image. Given the closeness of this relationship, the female spectator's desire can be described only in terms of a kind of narcissism – the female look demands a becoming.[2]

In celebrating Mrs Ramsay's beauty – her femininity – Lily is forced to negotiate her own relation to the spectacle of Mrs Ramsay as some form of narcissism. She cannot pay tribute to Mrs Ramsay as female without confronting the question of her own gender, and its identity with Mrs Ramsay's.

The relationship between Lily and Mrs Ramsay is over-determined (there are many factors coming into play). Firstly, there is the relation of spectator to spectacle; secondly, of artist to model; thirdly, of mourner to the person mourned; and fourthly, of daughter to mother. No wonder, then, that this relationship is the crux of the novel. There is so much at stake.

Mark Spilka notes that Lily's 'reactions to Mrs Ramsay are like those of an actual daughter once removed.'[3] We are justified, therefore, in using terms originally intended to describe the relationship of mother and daughter, to analyse that between Mrs Ramsay and Lily. Narcissism (the term of the relationship between female spectator and feminine spectacle) coincides fatally with identification (the term of the relationship between mother and daughter). Girls learn to be women through a complex process of imitation, assessment, and rejection of the women who mother them.

> A girl tends to retain elements of her preoedipal primary love and primary identification. This has been compounded through the years by reinforcement from a more conscious gender-role identification with her mother. The ease of this identification and the feeling of continuity with her mother conflict with a girl's felt need to separate from her and to overcome her ambivalent and dependent preoedipally-toned relationship.[4]

Lily's struggles with her own gender are compounded by her entrapment in a narcissistic spectatorial relationship with the object of her identification. In order to achieve separation, she must also renounce a certain measure of pleasure in Mrs Ramsay: she must admit that Mrs Ramsay is not wholly to be admired, and, consequently, that femininity is not necessarily a good thing. In making such an admission she runs the risk of inadvertently condemning herself as a woman, if she rejects femininity altogether. Her task then is to find some relation to Mrs Ramsay which partakes of narcissism and identification without being completely governed by them.

Lily's problem initially is to do with the relations between men and women. This is not a question of their composition in the picture, but rather of the conditions of production of the work of art itself. Mr Ramsay like Tansley earlier threatens to distract Lily's attention and compromise her vision: 'as if any interruption would break the frail shape she was building on the table she turned her back to the window lest Mr Ramsay should see her' (TL, 138). The hazards of interruption and exposure are as frequent as they were in Part I, but now Mr Ramsay's attempt to repeat his experience with his wife, when he came to her for sympathy as she sat in the window, seems doomed to failure. This is part of the force of Mr Ramsay's ' "you will find us much changed" ' (TL, 139), for in fact he has not changed, but the system of relations in which he finds himself has. In the end the regression into the past ('as she dipped into the blue paint, she dipped too into the past there' [TL, 160]) confirms its supersession by a changed present. Lily thinks of Mrs Ramsay: 'one would have to say to her, It has all gone against your wishes. They're happy like that; I'm happy like this. Life has changed completely' (TL, 162). It seems that the power of Mrs Ramsay's beauty and of her will was not in fact as irresistible as it seemed. Her vision – her view of how things should be – has now been dimmed by death. Lily feels a certain satisfaction in thinking that she knows and sees things of which Mrs Ramsay has no inkling. 'Oh the dead! she murmured, one pitied them, one brushed them aside, one had even a little contempt for them. They are at our mercy. Mrs Ramsay has faded and gone, she thought. We can over-ride her wishes, improve away her limited, old-fashioned ideas' (TL, 162).

Yet this is not entirely true. While Mr Ramsay lives there is still a force pulling Lily backwards into the past, obliging her to fill the gap that Mrs Ramsay has left. It becomes clear that femininity is not simply to do with appearance: it is also an activity, a particular function in an emotional and social con-figuration. Mr Ramsay is not particularly impressed by Lily's looks, any more than his wife was: 'she seemed to have shrivelled slightly, he thought. She looked a little skimpy, wispy' (TL, 141). But in spite of Lily's falling far short of his wife's beauty, her saturated womanliness, Mr Ramsay is pre-pared to approach Lily, impelled by 'an enormous need . . . to approach any woman, to force them, he did not care how, his need was so great, to give him what he wanted: sympathy' (TL, 142). Lily's failure to respond – her inability to take up her place in the heterosexual system set up by the Ramsays many years before – seems to outlaw her from womanhood: 'any other woman in the whole world would have done some-thing, said something – all except myself, thought Lily, gird-ing at herself bitterly, who am not a woman, but a peevish, ill-tempered, dried-up old maid presumably' (TL, 142). Being a woman is a matter of maintaining a particular set of relations. The problem with Lily is that the relations in which she is interested are on her canvas, and not on the terrace. What she wants is to be left alone. But the proximity of Mr Ramsay challenges the primacy of the relations in her picture: 'She could not see the colour; she could not see the lines; even with his back turned to her, she could only think, But he'll be down on me in a moment' (TL, 140). Rage distorts her vision, re-moves from her what she cannot do without: her painter's eye. For the moment painting and femininity seem irreconcilable.

The problem is one of a kind of emotional tyranny. 'This was tragedy – not palls, dust, and the shroud; but children

coerced, their spirits subdued' (TL, 140). The younger generation must fight their way out of the old picture and into a new
one. But they are always threatened – as the house itself was in
Part I – with floods which are simultaneously the waters of
chaos and of the past. Mr Ramsay is like a tidal wave – 'this
enormous flood of grief' (TL, 142) – on which Lily should be
able to ride: 'she ought to have floated off instantly upon some
wave of sympathetic expansion: the pressure on her was
tremendous' (TL, 142). But Lily is fastidiously concerned to
avoid this wave of passion: 'all she did, miserable sinner that
she was, was to draw her skirts a little closer round her ankles,
lest she should get wet' (TL, 143). It is once again boots that
save her (the crunch of Mrs McNab's boots on the shingle
signalled the reclaiming of the house from decay in Part II). Lily
praises Mr Ramsay's boots, and at once 'his palls, his drap-
eries, his infirmities fell from him' (TL, 144). Lily has recalled
his thoughts to the substance that has always so pleased him,
and at once they arrive at the safety of the shore, 'a sunny
island where peace dwelt, sanity reigned and the sun for ever
shone, the blessed island of good boots' (TL, 144).

Mr Ramsay's pleasure is a cue for Lily's response. 'She felt
her eyes swell and tingle with tears' (TL, 144). But he is no
longer in need of her – a part of her unfitness is that she
should be out of phase – so that she is left with feelings which
can find no issue: 'She felt a sudden emptiness; a frustration'
(TL, 145). It is under the influence of this feeling that she
begins to paint, so that her painting becomes a reaction to
feelings out of context, excess emotion without a suitable
relation: exactly the dilemma of grief. Mr Ramsay's departure
– she thinks of 'what, now that they were off, she would not
have the chance of giving him' (TL, 145) – while of course far
less threatening than Mrs Ramsay's, provokes the same problem, 'this folly and waste of emotion' (TL, 147) for people
who are no longer there. But her successful achievement of
the appropriate feminine emotion – sympathy – allows her to
return to a narcissistic celebration of Mrs Ramsay, because,
temporarily, she is in harmony with her.

Lily's triumph is her simultaneous conception of the lines on her canvas, and the relations between people. She brings them into focus together so that they suddenly seem like the same problem. Woolf's friends Roger Fry and Charles Mauron, an art critic and a novelist, had also sought a common vocabulary for the arrangement of space in the visual arts and in literature. Mauron defined it as follows:

> What analogue in literature shall we give to volume? It suffices to transfer it from the domain of space to that of the spirit; and as the notion of volume admits of all spatial possibilities, the corresponding literary notion ought to admit of all spiritual possibilities.[5]

In order to think through her picture, Lily must think through the system of relations in which she finds her own identity. Like the film-maker, she must understand the position of the spectator before she can evolve her art.

What Lily does is to substitute her activities in relation to her picture, for those that Mrs Ramsay directed at her family. If she continues to operate in Mrs Ramsay's way, but on a different object, she remains within the narcissistic/identificatory relationship, while nonetheless allowing herself the freedom to act in a way of which Mrs Ramsay would not have approved. The 'fountain' with which Mrs Ramsay responded to her husband's demands is now an image for Lily's rhythmic stroking of her canvas, in an echo also of the lighthouse beam: 'her mind kept throwing up from its depths, scenes, and names, and sayings, and memories and ideas, like a fountain spurting over that glaring, hideously difficult white space, while she modelled it with greens and blues' (TL, 149). The movement of Lily's body is dictated by some inherent pattern in what she sees, 'some rhythm which was dictated to her (she kept looking at the hedge, at the canvas) by what she saw' (TL, 149). The successful realisation of shape on the canvas is the transfer of some dynamic relation from the world of perception to the world of art.

The artist's problem, like that of Mrs Ramsay, whom Lily

remembers sitting on the beach, is one of identification, finding the rhythm: 'Mrs Ramsay sat and wrote letters by a rock. She wrote and wrote. "Oh," she said, looking up at last at something floating in the sea, "is it a lobster pot? Is it an upturned boat?" ' (TL, 149). Lily painting her picture is also preoccupied with such a problem: 'yes, that is their boat, Lily Briscoe decided, standing on the edge of the lawn' (TL, 158). The key to Mrs Ramsay's art, which produces Lily's ('she brought together this and that and then this, and so made . . . this scene on the beach . . . which survived, after all these years, complete' [TL, 150]), is to rest in the rhythm of vision and emotion without seeking (as Mr Ramsay would) to understand it, to fashion a narrative for it: 'Mrs Ramsay sat silent. She was glad, Lily thought, to rest in silence, uncommunicative; to rest in the extreme obscurity of human relationships. Who knows what we are, what we feel?' (TL, 159). Lily thus feels her artistic endeavours to be a part of her feminine inheritance: both she and Mrs Ramsay are concerned to produce composed and harmonious scenes. But she deviates from Mrs Ramsay's model in her rejection of the beauty which, as we have seen, froze male admirers into a fetishistic and dishonest gaze. While identifying with Mrs Ramsay's role as the maker of 'something permanent' (TL, 151), she explicitly distances herself from a narcissistic relation to Mrs Ramsay's beauty by an onslaught on her appearance as a source of falsity and paralysis.

Lily's dissatisfaction with Mrs Ramsay is imaged as a distaste at the way in which her beauty is framed.

> Beauty had this penalty – it came too readily, came too completely. It stilled life – froze it. One forgot the little agitations; the flush, the pallor, some queer distortion, some light or shadow, which made the face unrecognizable for a moment and yet added a quality one saw for ever after. (TL, 164–5)

Lily's frustration is with the easy reproducibility of Mrs Ramsay's beauty, like the mass production of the film still. The French critic Roland Barthes uses similar terms to describe the film image of Garbo's face. It represented an 'essential beauty', 'which could be neither reached nor renounced.'[6] Female admirers of it could only feel their own inadequacy, while deriving pleasure from the celebration of the femininity in which they too participated.

Lily's resistance to Mrs Ramsay's beauty comes from her sense that it paralyses, is itself paralysed, rather than its being something that sets in motion (as the 'woman-structure' usually expects of women). Lily wants a motion picture, rather than a still, to be the best expression of Mrs Ramsay's beauty. As it is, it is the framed image which is memorable (when Mrs Ramsay comes back, she reappears in the window), and so, while Lily's picture is ideally suited to capture the momentary nature of its subject's appeal, Mrs Ramsay's beauty, like Garbo's face, resists any attempt to produce it as narrative. Barthes notes that Garbo went to peculiar pains with veils and cloaks to conceal her aging – her body's narrative – from the world. 'The face of Garbo is an Idea, that of [Audrey] Hepburn an Event.'[7] But this means that it is Mrs Ramsay's beauty, as an image of arrest, that Lily must reject if she wants to move onwards and to realise her own gender as an experience of possibility, as something that continually *happens*. Her final line down the centre of the picture could be an obliteration of Mrs Ramsay as spectacle and as Idea: a decision to turn aside from the framed beauty which has constrained the possibilities for femininity throughout the book.

Mrs Ramsay's beauty is unsatisfactory because it is more like a mask than like an expression of inner movement. Because of this, Lily's difficulty is with the representation of feminine emotional rhythm. 'How could one express in words these emotions of the body? express that emptiness there?' (TL, 165). The movement of her paint brush exactly records the fluctuations of emotion: 'with a curious physical sensation, as if she were urged forward and at the same time must hold herself back, she made her first quick decisive stroke' (TL, 148). But the absence of Mrs Ramsay produces a physical sensation which is not easily translated into the movements of the painting arm, 'a hardness, a hollowness, a strain' (TL, 165). The sense of a focal point is denied: 'the whole wave and whisper of the garden became like curves and arabesques flourishing round a centre of complete emptiness' (TL, 166). Finally Lily's emotion is expressible not within the painting, but in its own terms, that is, as a physical rather than an aesthetic crisis, and one that is conventionally specifically feminine: she weeps (TL, 166). This spasm of sorrow initiates the process of rejection which will end with her abandonment of the representation of essential feminine beauty as an aesthetic and an autobiographical project.

The emphasis in Part III is on the younger generation and their assessment of their parents' (or their surrogate parents') personalities, lives and relationships. Where the kaleidoscope was the mechanism associated with Part I, Part III is like looking through the wrong end of a telescope. We have been prepared for this in Part II, with the wandering projection of Mrs Ramsay's image on the wall (TL, 127). The nearer the boat moves to the lighthouse, the smaller and more irrelevant Mrs Ramsay begins to look, as Cam and James are increasingly preoccupied with their father (from p. 169 onwards).

In Part I, the rhythmic flash of the lighthouse was associated with Mrs Ramsay's pleasure. Among other things, the lighthouse represents the possibility of sexual satisfaction for women, and therefore, one of the sources of masculine self-satisfaction.

> So it was like that, James thought, the Lighthouse one had seen across the bay all these years; it was a stark tower on a bare rock. It satisfied him. It confirmed some obscure feeling of his about his own character. (TL, 187)

The stark loneliness of the lighthouse speaks to James of his own gender and provokes apparently irrelevant thoughts about the chatter of women:

> Old Mrs Beckwith, for example, was always saying how nice it

was and how sweet it was and how they ought to be so proud
and they ought to be so happy, but as a matter of fact James
thought, looking at the Lighthouse stood there on its rock, it's
like that. (TL, 187)

The truth of sexual relations is nothing like the sentimental
gathering-round of women. It is rather the impenetrable isolation in which the men on the lighthouse live, and the monolith
of biological sex – the inflexibility symbolised in the paralys-
ing effect of Mrs Ramsay's beauty.

As James approaches the lighthouse, he feels himself
resolved in sympathy with his father, who 'looked as if he had
become physically what was always at the back of both their
minds – that loneliness which was for both of them the truth
about things' (TL, 186). Steering the boat, James takes on the
burden of manhood, the classic judicial role. Cam recognises
this: 'James the lawgiver, with the tablets of eternal wisdom
laid open on his knee (his hand on the tiller had become symbolical to her)' (TL, 157). Together, Mr Ramsay and James
enter the masculine conspiracy to judge, complete with props,
pipes and watches: 'having lighted his pipe [Mr Ramsay] took
out his watch. He looked at it attentively; he made, perhaps,
some mathematical calculation. At last he said, triumphantly:
"Well done!" ' (TL, 189). Even the somnolent Carmichael is
prevailed upon to give both approval and blessing, 'looking
like an old pagan God, shaggy, with weeds in his hair and the
trident (it was only a French novel) in his hand' (TL, 191).

> He stood there spreading his hands over all the weakness and
> suffering of mankind; [Lily] thought he was surveying, toler-
> antly, compassionately, their final destiny. Now he has
> crowned the occasion, she thought, when his hands slowly fell,
> as if she had seen him let fall from his great height a wreath of
> violets and asphodels which, fluttering slowly, lay at length
> upon the earth. (TL, 191)

Carmichael's action brings together not only the judicial
tendencies of the men in the book, but also the beauty and
mortality of the women. Tansley has imagined Mrs Ramsay
with 'wild violets' (TL, 18) in her hair; Lily imagines Prue's

death as a Persephone-like gesture of dropping her flowers: 'she let her flowers fall from her basket, scattered and tumbled them on to the grass' (TL, 185). The flowers that Prue drops could almost be her bridal wreath (we remember that love carries with it 'the seeds of death' [TL, 93]). Mr Carmichael, seeming to scatter violets on the grass, is presiding over humanity's 'final destiny', the inescapability of sexual difference and the closeness of femininity to castration and therefore to death.

As Cam looks back at the house and the island, they begin to look like the landscape of her past: 'she was thinking how all those paths and the lawn, thick and knotted with the lives they had lived there, were gone: were rubbed out' (TL, 155). For distance, like Lily's picture, can erase. Cam hardly seems to remember her mother; she is preoccupied with the present, with finding a satisfactory relation to both the father she remembers and the father she knows. For James, the problem of the relation with his father is bound up with memories of his mother, with 'a flash of blue' (TL, 157). The tunnel vision of this part of the book – its relatively constricted perspectives (it is only possible to look along one plane, between the house and the lighthouse) – is a result of looking backwards, of discovering that to go out to the lighthouse is also to go deeper and deeper back into the past.

As Cam begins to assess the doubleness of her feeling for her father, she escapes not only the tyranny of the past but also the feeling of her father's tyranny itself. 'He was not vain nor a tyrant' (TL, 175). With the mellowing of her attitude towards him, she comes into her inheritance of images previously associated with her mother and heterosexual femininity: 'from her hand, ice cold, held deep in the sea, there spurted up a fountain of joy at the change, at the escape, at the adventure (that she should be alive, that she should be there)' (TL, 174). Cam, like Lily, reproduces her mother's idioms without necessarily acquiescing to her mother's role.

What Cam escapes is a past and a present shadowed by the despotism of death, expressed through Mr Ramsay's thoughtless bullying. At first his chanting of poetry on the boat 'shocked her – it outraged her' (TL, 155). But finally she finds herself repeating her father's words as an incantation which comforts and protects: 'about here, she thought, dabbling her fingers in the water, a ship had sunk, and she murmured dreamily, half asleep, how we perished, each alone' (TL, 176). Mourning is now not a shock or an outrage, the wrecking of ships and lives, but a nostalgic echo that can set the mind free. James and Cam, feeling this, are surprised to find that suddenly death seems to have become a commonplace for Mr Ramsay as well. They pass a spot where men were drowned.

> And Mr Ramsay taking a look at the spot was about, James and Cam were afraid, to burst out:
>
> But I beneath a rougher sea,
>
> and if he did, they could not bear it; they would shriek aloud; they could not endure another explosion of the passion that boiled in him; but to their surprise all he said was 'Ah' as if he thought to himself, But why make a fuss about that? Naturally men are drowned in a storm, but it is a perfectly straightforward affair, and the depths of the sea (he sprinkled the crumbs from his sandwich paper over them) are only water after all. (TL, 189)

The fanciful scattering of flowers with which Lily has imagined the deaths of Mrs Ramsay and Prue is displaced by Mr Ramsay's far more prosaic scattering of bread, in a parody of burial at sea which emphasises life and nourishment rather than death and decay.

Mr Ramsay's despotism is recognised most clearly by James. Mrs Ramsay's final departure in death is conflated by James with her momentary lapse of attention when his father called her away. That routine deprivation becomes an image for the monstrous absence of the dead, and Mr Ramsay – or something to do with him – is held responsible for both.

> Only now, as he grew older, and sat staring at his father in an impotent rage, it was not him, that old man reading, whom he wanted to kill, but it was the thing that descended on him –

without his knowing it perhaps: that fierce sudden black-winged harpy. (TL, 170)

This is the beginning of James' dissociation of the rhetoric of death from the far less sublime reality of his father's aging body. His father's unexpectedly simply ' "Ah" ' at the end is an expression of the same purging and reduction of language. Rather than being death-dealing, Mr Ramsay is gradually seen to be just another of death's victims.

By the time they arrive at the lighthouse the terms of the exchange between James and Cam, and Mr Ramsay, have shifted from 'tyranny, despotism' (TL, 170) to an economy of the gift. 'What do you want? they both wanted to ask. They both wanted to say, Ask us anything and we will give it you. But he did not ask them anything' (TL, 190). Lily, too, shifts from being wanted by Mr Ramsay to wanting him: 'whatever she had wanted to give him, when he left her that morning, she had given him at last' (TL, 191). The novel's climax is this transformation of Mr Ramsay from the subject of desire into its object.

Lily's impatient brush-stroke allows her to go beyond femininity as an aesthetic ideal, by either obliterating or completing Mrs Ramsay as spectacle. This frees her into being able to distinguish between some acceptable elements of her feminine role (finding herself suddenly able to be generous to Mr Ramsay), and others which she can now reject (marriage, children, the renunciation of her commitment to her art).

Jane Lilienfeld believes the novel is a surpassing of Mrs Ramsay:

> Lily Briscoe's initiation into womanhood is the process by which she turns from the stranglehold of the archetype to an understanding that she may forge her own patterns of behaviour which allow her spirit to achieve an independence and maturity unhoped for in her early fierce ambivalence.[8]

This is not wholly so. In fact the novel ends in agreement with Mrs Ramsay's view of things: Mr Ramsay leaps onto the lighthouse rock 'like a young man' (TL, 191), echoing Mrs

Ramsay's earlier delight in him; Lily is 'relieved' like Mrs Ramsay at having given him something (TL, 191). Mr Ramsay has taken his wife's place as the object of desire for the novel, such that Lily, in the end, is in agreement with Mrs Ramsay in her longing for Mr Ramsay. Lily rejects not what Mrs Ramsay did, but how she looked (she endorses identification rather than narcissism). She has been moving towards this throughout the novel. Bankes sees in her picture that: 'mother and child then – objects of universal veneration, and in this case the mother was famous for her beauty – might be reduced, he pondered, to a purple shadow without irreverence' (TL, 52). Finally Lily acquiesces to some of her duties within the system of gender relations bequeathed to her, in her willingness to offer Mr Ramsay sympathy. What she rejects is the spectatorial – narcissistic – position offered to her. In finishing her picture she at once relinquishes the pleasure of contemplating Mrs Ramsay's beauty, and escapes the discomfort of seeing herself simultaneously realised, and unrealised, in what she sees. It is not unlike the transition described by Barthes from the fetishising gaze at Garbo, to the more detached attention given to the face of Hepburn who, in being variously herself rather than achieved archetype, renounces all demand on the spectator to become like her.

> The face of Audrey Hepburn, for instance, is individualised, not only because of its peculiar thematics (woman as child, woman as kitten) but also because of her person, of an almost unique specification of the face, which has nothing of the essence left in it, but is constituted by an infinite complexity of morphological functions.[9]

Although both women are beyond imitation, Garbo, by staging femininity as a concept, places an implicit demand on her female spectator which Hepburn, representing only herself, does not. It is this demand – this transfixing of the attention – which Lily refuses.

We have seen that Woolf felt freed by the writing of *To the Lighthouse*. Sara Ruddick associates that relief with the feelings described in 'Professions for women' about the 'angel in the house'.[10] 'It was not necessary for me to depend solely on charm for my living', says Woolf, and tells how, because of that economic freedom, she turned on the spectre of the woman who lives for men and killed her in herself.[11] But it is not clear, in fact, that Lily accomplishes such a task. What she kills is the complicated narcissism with which she approached Mrs Ramsay. Doing that frees her to live her femininity as both inheritance and innovation. This is, in the end, feminism's only possible condition of existence.

Notes

PREFACE

1. Hélène Cixous, 'The laugh of the Medusa', in *New French Feminisms: An anthology*, edited and with introductions by Elaine Marks and Isabelle de Courtivron (New York: Schocken, 1981), pp. 245–64 (p. 253).

HISTORICAL AND CULTURAL CONTEXT

1. Leonard Woolf, *Beginning Again: An autobiography of the years 1911–1918* (London: Hogarth, 1964), p. 21.
2. *Ibid.*, p. 25.
3. Raymond Williams, 'The Bloomsbury fraction' (1978), in *Problems in Materialism and Culture: Selected essays* (London: Verso, 1980), pp. 148–69 (p. 155).
4. Virginia Woolf, 'Mr. Bennett and Mrs. Brown', in *Collected Essays*, 4 vols. (London: Hogarth, 1966–7), I, pp. 319–37 (p. 332).
5. Virginia Woolf, 'Modern fiction', in *op. cit.*, II, pp. 103–10 (p. 107); 'Dorothy Richardson', in *Virginia Woolf: Women and writing*, edited by Michèle Barrett (London: Women's Press, 1979), pp. 188–92 (p. 191).
6. Virginia Woolf, 'Modern fiction', *op. cit.*, p. 107.
7. Kate Flint, 'Virginia Woolf and the General Strike', *Essays in Criticism*, **36** (1986), pp. 319–34.
8. Virginia Woolf, *A Room of One's Own*, 1929 (London: Triad/ Granada, 1977), p. 70.
9. Leonard Woolf, *op. cit.*, p. 172.

Notes

CRITICAL RECEPTION OF THE TEXT

1. *Times Literary Supplement*, 5 May 1927, p. 315.
2. Reprinted in *Virginia Woolf: The Critical Heritage*, edited by Robin Majumdar and Allen McLaurin (London: Routledge, 1975), pp. 204–5 (p. 204).
3. Rachel A. Taylor, *Spectator*, 14 May 1927, p. 871, reprinted in Majumdar and McLaurin (eds.), *op. cit.*, pp. 198–200 (p. 199).
4. Muriel Bradbrook, 'Notes on the style of Mrs. Woolf', *Scrutiny* 1 (1932), 33–8. Beja describes in the introduction to *Virginia Woolf 'To the Lighthouse': A casebook* (London: Macmillan, 1970) how Bradbrook turned down his request to reprint her article (p. 20).
5. W. H. Mellers, 'Mrs. Woolf and life', *Scrutiny*, 6 (1937), pp. 71–5; F. R. Leavis, 'After *To the Lighthouse*', *Scrutiny*, 10 (1942), pp. 295–8 (295).
6. Q. D. Leavis, 'Caterpillars of the commonwealth unite!', *Scrutiny*, 7 (1938), 203–14.
7. E. M. Forster, *Virginia Woolf* (Cambridge: Cambridge University Press, 1942), p. 28.
8. Arnold Kettle, *An Introduction to the English Novel*, 2 vols., 1951–3 (2nd edn, London: Hutchinson, 1967) II, p. 94.
9. Bradbrook, *op. cit.*, p. 38.
10. Joseph L. Blotner, 'Mythic patterns in *To the Lighthouse*' *PMLA*, 71 (1956) 547–62, reprinted in Beja, *op. cit.*, pp. 169–88 (pp. 171, 172).
11. Glenn Pedersen, 'Vision in *To the Lighthouse*', *PMLA*, 73 (1958), pp. 585–600 (585).
12. Keith May, 'The symbol of "painting" in Virginia Woolf's *To the Lighthouse*', *A Review of English Literature*, 8 (1967), 91–8; Harold Fromm, '*To the Lighthouse*: music and sympathy', *English Miscellany*, 19 (1968), 181–95.
13. Geoffrey Hartman, 'Virginia's web', in *Beyond Formalism: Literary essays 1958–1970* (New Haven: Yale University Press, 1970), pp. 71–84.
14. Annis Pratt, 'Sexual imagery in *To the Lighthouse*: a new feminist approach', *Modern Fiction Studies*, 18 (1972), 417–31 (422).
15. Sara Ruddick, 'Learning to live with the angel in the house', *Women's Studies*, 4 (1977), 181–200; Jane Lilienfeld, ' "The deceptiveness of beauty": mother love and mother hate in *To the Lighthouse*', *Twentieth-Century Literature*, 23 (1977), 345–76.

16. Delia Donahue, *The Novels of Virginia Woolf* (Rome: Bulzoni, 1977), p. 109.
17. Robert Caserio, *Plot, Story and the Novel: From Dickens and Poe to the modern period* (Princeton: Princeton University Press, 1979).
18. Gayatri Chakravorty Spivak, 'Unmaking and making in *To the Lighthouse*', in *Women and Language in Literature and Society*, edited by Sally McConnell-Ginet, Ruth Borker and Nelly Furman (New York: Praeger, 1980), pp. 310–27.
19. Maria Dibattista, *Virginia Woolf's Major Novels: The fables of anon* (New Haven: Yale University Press, 1980), p. 108.
20. Gillian Beer, 'Hume, Stephen and elegy in *To the Lighthouse*', *Essays in Criticism*, **34** (1984), 33–55.
21. Kate Flint, 'Virginia Woolf and the General Strike', *Essays in Criticism*, **36** (1986), 319–34.

THEORETICAL PERSPECTIVES

1. Muriel Bradbrook, 'Notes on the Style of Mrs. Woolf', *Scrutiny*, **1** (1932), 33–8 (38).
2. *Ibid.*, 38.
3. Glenn Pedersen, 'Vision in *To the Lighthouse*', *PMLA*, **73** (1958), 585–600 (587).
4. *Ibid.*, 588.
5. L. C. Knights and Donald Culver, 'A Manifesto', *Scrutiny*, **I** (1932), 2–7 (3, 5).
6. Arnold Kettle, *An Introduction to the English Novel*, 2 vols., 1951–3 (2nd edn, London: Hutchinson, 1967) II, p. 94.
7. Michèle Barrett, 'Introduction', in *Virginia Woolf: Women and writing* (London: Women's Press, 1979), p. 5.
8. Harold Bloom, *The Anxiety of Influence* (Oxford: Oxford University Press, 1973), p. 30.
9. Perry Meisel, *The Absent Father: Virginia Woolf and Walter Pater* (New Haven: Yale University Press, 1980), p. 33.
10. Bloom, *op. cit.*, p. 39.
11. Rachel Bowlby, *Virginia Woolf: Feminist destinations* (Oxford: Basil Blackwell, 1988), pp. 65, 68.
12. Bowlby, *ibid.*, p. 71.
13. Nancy Chodorow, *The Reproduction of Mothering: Psychoanalysis and the sociology of gender* (Berkeley, Los Angeles: University of California Press, 1978), pp. 192–3.

14. Gayatri Chakravorty Spivak, 'Unmaking and making in *To the Lighthouse*', in *Women and Language in Literature and Society*, edited by Sally McConnell-Ginet, Ruth Borker and Nelly Furman (New York: Praeger, 1980), pp. 310–27 (p. 310).
15. Jacques Lacan, *The Four Fundamental Concepts of Psycho-Analysis*, edited by Jacques-Alain Miller, translated by Alan Sheridan (New York: Norton, 1981), p. 20.
16. Spivak, *op. cit.*, p. 311.
17. Spivak, *op. cit.*, p. 311.
18. Spivak, *op. cit.*, p. 311.
19. Toril Moi. *Sexual/Textual Politics: Feminist literary theory* (London: Routledge, 1985), p. 16.
20. Moi, *ibid.*, p. 9.
21. Moi, *ibid.*, p. 10.

1. GHOSTS

1. Virginia Woolf, *'To the Lighthouse': The original holograph draft*, transcribed and edited by Susan Dick (London: Hogarth, 1983), Appendix A, p. 11.
2. Dick, *ibid.*, p. 2.
3. Jeanne Schulkind, 'Introduction', in *Moments of Being: Unpublished autobiographical writings*, Virginia Woolf (London: Triad/Granada, 1978), pp. 13–28 (p. 15).
4. Dick, *op. cit.*, p. 2.
5. Leslie Stephen to Charles Eliot Norton, 28 June 1895, quoted in *Sir Leslie Stephen's Mausoleum Book*, introduced and edited by Alan Bell (Oxford: Clarendon, 1977), p. x.
6. Leslie Stephen to Julia Stephen, 4 September 1884, quoted in *ibid.*, p. xx.
7. Phyllis Rose, 'Mrs. Ramsay and Mrs. Woolf', *Women's Studies*, 1 (1973), 199–216 (212).

2. PERSPECTIVES

1. Virginia Woolf, 'Modern Fiction', in *Collected Essays*, 4 vols. (London: Hogarth, 1966–7), II, pp. 103–10 (p. 106).

Notes

2. Virginia Woolf, 'To the Lighthouse': The original holograph draft, transcribed and edited by Susan Dick (London: Hogarth, 1983), p. 57.
3. Dick, ibid., p. 2.
4. For details of the variants between the two editions, see J. A. Lavin, 'The first editions of To the Lighthouse', Proof, 2 (1972), 185–211.
5. Virginia Woolf, To the Lighthouse (New York: Harcourt Brace, 1927), p. 194.
6. John Mepham, 'Figures of desire: narration and fiction in To the Lighthouse', in The Modern English Novel: The reader, the writer and the work, edited by Gabriel Josipovici (London: Open Books, 1976), pp. 149–85 (p. 155).

3. READING ALOUD

1. Gillian Beer, 'Hume, Stephen and elegy in To the Lighthouse', Essays in Criticism, 34 (1984), 33–55 (42).
2. Mary Ann Doane, 'Film and the masquerade: theorising the female spectator', Screen, 23 (1982), 74–87 (76).
3. Thorstein Veblen, The Theory of the Leisure Class, 1899 (Harmondsworth: Penguin, 1979), p. 75.
4. Laura Mulvey, 'Visual pleasure and narrative cinema', Screen, 16 (1975), 6–18 (11).
5. Mulvey, ibid., 8–9.
6. Mulvey, ibid., 6, 7.
7. Mulvey, ibid., 13.
8. Mulvey, ibid., 13.
9. Sigmund Freud, On Sexuality, translated by James Strachey, edited by Angela Richards, Pelican Freud Library, VII (Harmondsworth: Penguin, 1977), p. 65.
10. Freud, ibid., p. 352.
11. Mulvey, op. cit., 13–14.
12. Stephen Heath, Questions of Cinema (London: Macmillan, 1981), p. 54.
13. Annette Kuhn, Women's Pictures: Feminism and cinema (London: Routledge, 1982), p. 53.
14. Kuhn, ibid., p. 49.
15. Heath, op. cit., p. 87.
16. Heath, op. cit., p. 87.
17. Heath, op. cit., p. 87.

18. Virginia Woolf, *'To the Lighthouse'*: *The original holograph draft*, transcribed and edited by Susan Dick (London: Hogarth, 1983), p. 2.
19. Makiko Minow-Pinkney, *Virginia Woolf and the Problem of the Subject: Feminine writing in the major novels* (Hemel Hempstead: Harvester Wheatsheaf, 1987), p. 93.
20. Mulvey, *op. cit.*, 13.
21. Annis Pratt, 'Sexual imagery in *To the Lighthouse*: a new feminist approach', *Modern Fiction Studies*, 18 (1972), 417–31 (420).
22. Pratt, *ibid.*, 420.
23. Pratt, *ibid.*, 426.
24. Freud, *op. cit.*, p. 356.
25. Freud, *op. cit.*, p. 356.
26. Freud, *op. cit.*, p. 353.
27. Doane, *op. cit.*, p. 78.

4. THE DINNER PARTY

1. Annette Kuhn, *Women's Pictures: Feminism and cinema* (London: Routledge, 1982), p. 32.
2. Kuhn, *ibid.*, p. 34.
3. Kuhn, *ibid.*, p. 34.
4. Maria Dibattista, *Virginia Woolf's Major Novels: The fables of anon* (New Haven: Yale University Press, 1980), pp. 84–5.
5. For a thorough analysis of the significance of colour in *To the Lighthouse*, see Jack F. Stewart, 'Colour in *To the Lighthouse*', *Twentieth-Century Literature*, 31 (1985), 438–58.
6. Gillian Beer, 'Hume, Stephen and elegy in *To the Lighthouse*', *Essays in Criticism*, 34 (1984), 33–55 (38–9).
7. Sigmund Freud, *On Sexuality*, translated by James Strachey and edited by Angela Richards, Pelican Freud Library, VII (Harmondsworth: Penguin, 1977), p. 372.
8. Stewart, *op. cit.*, 453.
9. Freud, *op. cit.*, pp. 354–5.

5. TIME PASSING

1. Makiko Minow-Pinkney, *Virginia Woolf and the Problem of the*

Subject: Feminine writing in the major novels (Hemel Hempstead: Harvester Wheatsheaf, 1987), p. 101.

2. Mary Ann Doane, 'Film and the masquerade: theorising the female spectator', *Screen,* **23** (1982), 74–87 (84).
3. Kate Flint, 'Virginia Woolf and the General Strike', *Essays in Criticism,* **36** (1986), 319–34.
4. Flint, *ibid.,* 329.
5. Minow-Pinkney, *op. cit.,* p. 102.

6. GETTING TO THE LIGHTHOUSE

1. Mitchell A. Leaska, *Virginia Woolf's Lighthouse: A study in critical method* (London: Hogarth, 1970), p. 112.
2. Mary Ann Doane, 'Film and masquerade: theorising the female spectator', *Screen,* **23** (1982), 74–87 (78).
3. Mark Spilka , *Virginia Woolf's Quarrel with Grieving* (Lincoln and London: University of Nebraska, 1980), p. 80.
4. Nancy Chodorow, *The Reproduction of Mothering: Psycho-analysis and the sociology of gender* (Berkeley, Los Angeles, London: University of California Press, 1978), p. 136.
5. Charles Mauron, *The Nature of Beauty in Art and Literature* (London: Hogarth, 1927), p. 66.
6. Roland Barthes, 'The face of Garbo', in *Mythologies* (1957), translated by Annette Lavers (London: Jonathan Cape, 1972), pp. 56–7 (pp. 57, 56).
7. Barthes, *ibid.,* p. 57.
8. Jane Lilienfeld, ' "The deceptiveness of beauty": mother love and mother hate in *To the Lighthouse'*, *Twentieth-Century Literature,* **23** (1977), 345–76 (347).
9. Barthes, *op. cit.,* p. 57.
10. See Sara Ruddick, 'Learning to live with the angel in the house', *Women's Studies,* **4** (1977), 181–200.
11. Virginia Woolf, 'Professions for women', in *Collected Essays,* 4 vols. (London: Hogarth, 1966–7), II, pp. 284–9 (p. 286).

Select Bibliography

WORKS BY VIRGINIA WOOLF

The Voyage Out	(1915)
Night and Day	(1919)
Jacob's Room	(1922)
Mrs. Dalloway	(1925)
To the Lighthouse	(1927)
Orlando: A biography	(1928)
A Room of One's Own	(1929)
The Waves	(1931)
The Years	(1937)
Three Guineas	(1938)
Between the Acts	(1941)

Collected Essays, 4 vols. (London: Hogarth, 1966–7).
  Among the most significant are 'Modern fiction', 'Mr. Bennett and Mrs. Brown', and 'How it strikes a contemporary'.
The Letters of Virginia Woolf, edited by Nigel Nicolson and Joanne Trautmann, 6 vols. (London: Chatto, 1975–80).
Moments of Being: Unpublished autobiograhical writings, edited by Jeanne Schulkind (London: Triad/Granada, 1978).
The Diary of Virginia Woolf, edited by Anne Olivier Bell, 5 vols. (London: Hogarth, 1977–84). Both the letters and the diaries have excellent indexes in each volume, so they can easily be used as reference works, as well as read straight through.
Virginia Woolf: Women and writing, edited by Michèle Barrett

(London: Women's Press, 1979). This is a collection of Woolf's essays on issues associated with women's writing, and on individual women writers.

'To the Lighthouse': *The original holograph draft*, transcribed and edited by Susan Dick (London: Hogarth, 1983).

BIOGRAPHICAL WORKS

Bell, Quentin, *Virginia Woolf: A biography*, 2 vols. (London: Hogarth, 1972).
By Virginia Woolf's nephew, this is the standard and most detailed biography.

Rose, Phyllis, *Woman of Letters: A life of Virginia Woolf* (Oxford: Oxford University Press, 1978).
Rose contends that previous biographers have missed the centrality of Woolf's feminist commitment to both her work and her life. She emphasises Woolf's relationships with women as a major source of support and energy. An exciting corrective to Bell's research.

CRITICAL WORKS

Auerbach, Erich, *Mimesis: The representation of reality in Western literature* (1946), translated by Willard Trask (Princeton: Princeton University Press, 1953).
This classic of literary criticism is a history of the representation of reality in Western literature from antiquity through to the twentieth century.

Beer, Gillian, 'Hume, Stephen, and elegy in *To the Lighthouse*', *Essays in Criticism,* **34** (1984), 33–55.
This article explores Virginia Woolf's relationship with Leslie Stephen, both as father and as philosopher. It contains very useful information on the intellectual background to the novel, as well as suggesting ways in which the novel operates as a part of Woolf's work of mourning for her parents.

Bowlby, Rachel, *Virginia Woolf: Feminist destinations* (Oxford: Basil Blackwell, 1988).
One of the most recent full-length studies of Woolf's work, this

book is also a clear introduction to Freudian theory and psychoanalytic criticism.

Clements, Patricia and Isobel Grundy, eds., *Virginia Woolf: New critical essays* (London: Vision, 1983).

Isobel Grundy's article on Woolf's choices of names for her characters is especially original, and well worth reading.

Flint, Kate, 'Virginia Woolf and the General Strike', *Essays in Criticism*, 36 (1986), 319–34.

An analysis of Woolf's political philosophy through her reactions, encoded in 'Time Passes', to the General Strike of 1926.

Guiguet, Jean, *Virginia Woolf and her Works*, translated by J. Stewart (London: Hogarth, 1962).

This monumental study, though rather rambling, nevertheless presents a compellingly romantic and thorough analysis of Woolf's *œuvre*.

Holtby, Winifred, *Virginia Woolf* (London: Wishart, 1932).

This, one of the earliest studies of Woolf's work, is indispensable reading if you are interested in the contemporary women's movement as a context for Woolf's work.

Lavin, J. A., 'The first editions of *To the Lighthouse*', *Proof*, 2 (1972), 185–211.

Used with Susan Dick's edition of the original manuscript of *To the Lighthouse*, this article makes it possible to discover at least some of Woolf's changes of mind as she worked on the novel.

Leaska, Mitchell A., *Virginia Woolf's Lighthouse: A study in critical method* (London: Hogarth, 1970).

A useful reference work containing statistical analysis of the language and structure of *To the Lighthouse*.

Majumdar, Robin and Allen McLaurin, eds., *Virginia Woolf: The Critical Heritage* (London: Routledge, 1975).

A collection of contemporary reviews of Woolf's books.

Marcus, Jane, ed., *New Feminist Essays on Virginia Woolf* (London: Macmillan, 1981); *Virginia Woolf: A feminist slant* (Lincoln, Nebraska: University of Nebraska, 1983).

These two books mark a decisive change in Woolf studies, looking at her as a deliberately feminist writer whose works bear traces of self-censorship rather than of failures of political awareness.

Meisel, Perry, *The Absent Father: Virginia Woolf and Walter Pater* (New Haven: Yale University Press, 1980).

This book studies Woolf's covert debt to late nineteenth-century Aestheticism.

Minow-Pinkney, Makiko, *Virginia Woolf and the Problem of the Subject: Feminine writing in the major novels* (Hemel Hempstead: Harvester Wheatsheaf, 1987).

This account of Woolf's novels is also a clear introduction to the sometimes baffling work of Julia Kristeva.

Pratt, Annis, 'Sexual imagery in *To the Lighthouse*: a new feminist approach', *Modern Fiction Studies*, **18** (1972), 417–31.
This article is worth reading even if you end up disagreeing with it. One of the most thoughtful accounts of the Ramsays' marriage.

Spivak, Gayatri Chakravorty, 'Unmaking and making in *To the Lighthouse*', in *Women and Language in Literature and Society*, edited by Sally McConnell-Ginet, Ruth Borker and Nelly Furman (New York: Praeger, 1980), pp. 310–27.
A significant and original discussion of language and desire in the novel.

Stewart, Jack F., 'Colour in *To the Lighthouse*', *Twentieth-Century Literature*, **31** (1985), 438–58.
An imaginative investigation of the significance of the use of colour in the novel.

Zwerdling, Alex, *Virginia Woolf and the Real World* (Berkeley, Los Angeles, London: University of California, 1986).
Discussion of individual novels is preceded by an account of the social context of the issues raised in them. Proof that Woolf was not only living in an ivory tower.

CULTURAL AND FILM THEORY

Doane, Mary Ann, 'Film and the masquerade: theorising the female spectator', *Screen*, **23** (1982), 74–87.
This article uses Joan Riviere's paper on femininity as masquerade (available in *Formations of Fantasy*, edited by Victor Burgin, James Donald and Cora Kaplan (London: Methuen, 1986)) to discuss the relation of the female spectator to images of femininity in film.

Freud, Sigmund, *On Sexuality*, translated by James Strachey, edited by Angela Richards, Pelican Freud Library, VII (Harmondsworth: Penguin, 1977).
This collection brings together many of Freud's most significant writings on gender and sexuality, including 'Fetishism' and 'Female sexuality'.

Heath, Stephen, *Questions of Cinema* (London: Macmillan, 1981).
This volume collects together Heath's significant and wide-ranging articles from the 1970s on many aspects of psycho-analysis and film theory.

Kuhn, Annette, *Women's Pictures: Feminism and cinema* (London: Routledge, 1982).
   This book gives a clear overview of developments in cinema theory, as well as offering important readings of old and new films. An excellent introduction to the subject.
Mulvey, Laura, 'Visual pleasure and narrative cinema', *Screen*, **16** (1975), 6–18.
   This very important article concentrates on the idealisation of the female star image and explains it in terms of Freud's theory of fetishism.
Williams, Raymond, *Problems in Materialism and Culture* (London: Verso, 1980).
   A collection of articles that is a good introduction to the work of this very widely read socialist critic.

Index

Index